GERMANY'S UNDERGROUND

GERMANY'S UNDERGROUND

by

ALLEN WELSH DULLES

with a new introduction by

PETER HOFFMANN

DA CAPO PRESS

Copyright © 1947 by Allen W. Dulles
Introduction copyright © 2000 by Peter Hoffmann

Library of Congress Cataloging in Publication Data on file

First Da Capo Press Edition 2000

Published by Da Capo Press
A Member of the Perseus Books Group
http://www.dacapopress.com

1   2   3   4   5   6   7   8   9   10——03   02   01   00   99

To

C. T. D.

*For her unfailing help
and encouragement*

Acknowledgment

I am indebted to three persons for helping me piece together and reduce to manageable proportions the mass of data on the German underground: Wolf Von Eckardt, Henry Hart, and Mrs. Elizabeth Parsons Klein. Several friends in Switzerland, Germany, and the United States were of invaluable assistance in the collection of the source material: Mrs. Mary Bancroft of Zurich, De-Witt C. Poole, Francis Miller, Gero von S. Gaevernitz, Edward Waetjen, Karl Brandt, Sam Harris, Miss Marie-Louise Sarre, Countess Freya von Moltke, and others. A number of officers formerly with our occupation forces in Germany and on the staff of the prosecution at the Nürnberg War Crimes Trials have given me valuable data.

Several persons, in addition to certain of those mentioned above, kindly looked over all or sections of the manuscript and made helpful suggestions, including Hamilton Fish Armstrong, Colonel Truman Smith, Gerhard P. Van Arkel, Frederick C. Kempner, Paul A. Kempner, Frederick Oppenheimer, Robert Baum-Jungk, Dr. Hans Schoenfeld, Herbert von Beckerath, and Wayne Nelson.

Hans Bernd Gisevius and Fabian von Schlabrendorff, both of whom figure prominently in the following pages, have told their own stories of their part in the conspiracy against

Hitler. These have already appeared in Swiss editions and will be republished here for the American reader. Both men, many months ago, prepared for me valuable memoranda regarding the plot, and on these, with their consent, I have drawn from time to time. To Gero von S. Gaevernitz, who is editing the story of Schlabrendorff, I am indebted for much valuable material, including the diary of Albrecht von Kessel, and for the permission which Frau von Hassell has kindly given to refer to the unique diary of her husband, Ambassador Ulrich von Hassell, which has now been published in Switzerland (*Vom andern Deutschland*, Atlantis Verlag, Zürich).

For the choice of material, for its evaluation, and for the judgments expressed, I myself assume responsibility.

Contents

Foreword

The 20th of July, 1944, is a significant date in German history. On that day a group of Germans made a last, desperate attempt to assassinate Hitler and to set up a government which, purged of all Nazis, would surrender unconditionally—if no better treatment could be obtained. The fate of hundreds of thousands of soldiers and civilians, Allied and German, depended on the bomb which the conspirators smuggled into Hitler's headquarters as the first step in their elaborate plan to destroy the Nazi regime. To this plan the conspirators had given the code name Walküre.

For some twenty months before this attempt on Hitler's life I had been in Switzerland in charge of the work there of the Office of Strategic Services, organized and directed by the dynamic and resourceful General William J. Donovan. My first and most important task was to find out what was going on in Germany. Among other things, Washington wanted to know who in Germany were really opposed to the Hitler regime and whether they were actively at work to overthrow it. As far as the outside world could see, it often seemed as though Hitler *had* succeeded in winning over, hypnotizing or terrorizing the entire German nation.

From Switzerland I was able to establish contact with the

German underground, and for many months before the culmination of the plot on July 20 I had kept in touch with those who were conspiring to rid Germany of the Nazis and the Nazi state. Couriers, risking their lives, went back and forth between Switzerland and Germany with reports of the conspirators' progress, and these reports reached me through secret channels I had developed. The last of these couriers never returned. He was caught and later executed. But it was he who brought the word that all the plans to eliminate Hitler were prepared, and that the men who would carry them out were ready. On July 13 I radioed from Bern to Washington that the plotters had sent me word "the next few weeks will be our last chance to demonstrate the determination of the Germans themselves to rid Germany of Hitler and his gang and establish a decent regime."

An assignment to work in Germany after V-E Day afforded me an opportunity to satisfy my intense curiosity about the entire plot and the people involved in it. Though Himmler had used all the resources and artifices of the Gestapo to track down anyone suspected of the least complicity, and several thousand people had been executed, there were a few survivors, and some of them I came to know intimately. Moreover, the Nazis were more thorough in destroying persons who might testify against them than in getting rid of the written record. The files of the Gestapo, the stenographic reports of the trials of conspirators, and other sources, yielded fascinating details about the plot and the plotters. Many additional facts are contained in the records of the Nürnberg Tribunal.

There *was* an anti-Nazi underground working in Germany, despite the general impression to the contrary. It developed out of heterogeneous groups that finally achieved a working unity and reached into the vitals of the army and the government services. Professional men, church and labor leaders, and high commanding officers on various fronts participated. Even Field Marshals Rommel and von Kluge finally had a share, but this was late in the day, when they saw that military victory had eluded them. But there were others of a very different moral fiber, both civilian and military, who were not opportunists and who had fought Hitlerism for many years.

The story of these anti-Nazi Germans who risked their lives deserves to be told. It is not merely a story of a plot. It is, indeed, incontrovertible proof that even in a totalitarian state the struggle for individual liberty does not cease. The knowledge that this was so in Nazi Germany can inspire all those who hope and work to build something better in the Germany of tomorrow.

Introduction

$\mathbf{A}$llen Welsh Dulles was born in Watertown, New York, on April 6, 1893, the third of the five children of a liberal Presbyterian minister; he died on January 30, 1969. His grandfather and an uncle were Secretaries of State, and his elder brother John Foster was Secretary of State from 1953 to 1959. His younger sister Eleanor made a name for herself as an economist and from 1952 to 1959 presided over the Berlin Desk at the State Department. Allen's career culminated in the directorship, from 1953 to 1961, of the most powerful Secret Service agency America had ever known.*

At Princeton Allen Dulles met people whom he saw again later in public service. After graduation, he went to Allahabad in India to teach English at the Ewing Christian College, and to travel in the Far East. After his return to America, he took a graduate degree in international relations, joined the diplomatic service in 1916, and received postings in Vienna and Berne during the First World War. At Berne in 1917 he was responsible for intelligence gathering. At the end of the war, the Dulles brothers wanted to be included in the American delegation to the Paris Peace Conference; their uncle, Secretary of State Robert Lansing, refused to oblige them, but they had other connections. John Foster attached himself to one of President

---

* *Who Was Who 1961–1970* (London: Adam & Charles Black, 1972); *Who Was Who in America with World Notables, vol. V, 1969–1973* (Chicago: Marquis); *Who's Who, 1973*; Leonard Mosley, *Dulles: A Biography of Eleanor, Allen, and John Foster Dulles and Their Family Network* (New York: Dell, 1979), pp. 13–24.

Wilsons's chief advisors. Allen served as a low-level advisor on the Commission for Central European Settlements.* Both brothers thought the terms forced upon Germany at Versailles (under threat of military occupation) were too harsh.†

Allen subsequently served in the State Department from 1922 to 1926, was a delegate to the International Conference on Arms Traffic at Geneva in 1925, and acquired a law degree by studying at night. He resigned in 1926 in order to practice law in New York with the firm in which John Foster worked, Sullivan & Cromwell. Allen then served as a legal advisor to the Preparatory Disarmament Commission at Geneva in 1926 and 1927, and to the American delegation at the General Disarmament Conference at Geneva in 1932 and 1933.‡ Thus he remained in contact with some of the most important leaders of commerce and industry, and with key functionaries in the State Department.

The Dulles brothers' interests in Europe, specifically in Germany, continued in the 1930s. They both knew French and German, and Sullivan & Cromwell represented important American clients in Germany. Allen was deeply concerned with what the Nazis were doing to the Jews and tried to move the State Department to intervene, and Sullivan & Cromwell to give assistance to their German-Jewish clients. But his coldly rational brother did not view the situation with alarm and seemed insensitive to the persecutions of the Jews. He reacted angrily to the suggestion that the firm was anti-Jewish but refused to close its operations in Germany until his partners, including his brother Allen, virtually forced him to do so.§

When war threatened to break out, John Foster opposed any American intervention, which was in part an expression of his dislike of President Roosevelt, his commitment to the Republican Party, and his active support for Thomas E. Dewey. Allen

* Who Was Who 1961–1970; Neal H. Petersen, ed., *From Hitler's Doorstep: The Wartime Intelligence Reports of Allen Dulles, 1942–1945*, p. 2.

† Petersen, p. 3.

‡ *Who Was Who in America with World Notables, vol. V, 1969–1973*; Petersen, p. 3.

§ Mosley, pp. 103–110; Petersen, p. 4.

strongly favored intervention,* and by 1940 was in contact with William J. Donovan, whom Roosevelt named head of the Office of Coordinator of Information in July 1941, which became known as the Office of Strategic Services (OSS) in June 1942.† In 1942, after the Japanese attack on Pearl Harbor and the German declaration of war on the United States, Allen Dulles became chief of the New York Office of the Coordinator of Information.‡ He refined his skills and utilized his far-flung connections for the craft of intelligence gathering. Just as American forces were landing in French Morocco, and the German army was responding by occupying the previously unoccupied southern part of France only hours before the German army sealed the French border with Switzerland, Dulles arrived by train in Berne on November 8, 1942 as the OSS station chief with the official title of Special Assistant to the Minister, who was Leland Harrison.§ He resided at Herrengasse 23, which bordered on a vineyard that enabled visitors to come and go unseen at night. His assignment was above all "to find out what was going on in Germany." Among other things—the standard sort of intelligence about armaments, supplies, morale, strategic intentions—the American government wanted to know "who in Germany were really opposed to the Hitler regime and whether they were actively at work to overthrow it."‖

The sources for intelligence proved to be abundant in Switzerland. There were, besides ordinary spies and traitors, exiles and expatriates, ecumenical church functionaries, businessmen, diplomats of countries which were either neutral or German satellites, and opponents of the Hitler government. As the outcome of the war became clearer, the Swiss government

* Petersen, p. 4.
† Mosley, pp. 111–115, 128, 137; Petersen, p. 4.
‡ Petersen, pp. 4–5.
§ Allen Welsh Dulles, *Germany's Underground* (New York: Macmillan, 1947), p. xi;
‖ Dulles, *Germany's Underground*, p. xi.

became more helpful, worrying more about the advance of communist regimes than about occupation by German forces.*

Most of the reports Dulles and his staff sent to OSS headquarters in Washington concerned military matters such as enemy formations, troop movements, bombing results, and the armaments industry. A substantial amount dealt with the underground anti-Hitler movements in France, Italy, the Balkans, Hungary, and Austria—all of which received Allied encouragement and support. Germany, the principal opponent of the Allies in Europe, naturally absorbed most of Dulles's attention. His best sources were his German-American assistant, Gero von Schulze Gaevernitz; three German military-intelligence (Abwehr) agents, Hans Bernd Gisevius, Eduard Waetjen, and Captain Theodor Strünck; a businessman, Eduard Schulte; and a German Foreign Office official, Fritz Kolbe. Kolbe, rebuffed by the British, was a passionate anti-Nazi who demanded nothing more in return for his assistance than the defeat of Hitler. From August 1943 he was the richest source of information for Dulles on German military matters and on policy, and on German relations with her satellites, Turkey and Japan.†

Both Kolbe and Gisevius provided Dulles with information on the German rocket (V1 and V2) program. In recommending Gisevius as a witness for the Nuremburg War Crimes Trial, Dulles wrote to Justice Robert Jackson that Gisevius had provided him with "clues which later helped toward the spotting of the German testing station at Peenemunde."‡ The German Resistance attracted perhaps Dulles's greatest interest. He sought and received detailed information from resistors of the Left, as well as of the conservative and military side.§

Germany's Underground deals with what Dulles found: German civilians and military men "who were not opportunists and who had fought Hitlerism for many years." He found that

* Petersen, pp. 6–7.
† Petersen, pp. 7–9.
‡ Dulles to Justice Robert Jackson, March 27, 1946, Library of Congress, R. H. Jackson Papers Box 102 file "Gisevius, Hans Bernd".
§ Petersen, p. 30.

"even in a totalitarian state the struggle for individual liberty does not cease," and he concluded that there was hope for the future of Germany "because Germans from within the Reich made the attempt to rid the world of Hitler," and that "upon their example and their ideas the Germans can build, if they choose, the road to democracy."*

Three major accounts from within the German Resistance were published in Switzerland in 1946: the diplomat Ulrich von Hassell's diaries covering the years 1938 to 1944; Hans Bernd Gisevius's account from inside the political police and the Abwehr; and Fabian von Schlabrendorff's account from the point of view of the Resistance group around Colonel Henning von Tresckow in the staff of the Army Group Center in Russia.† A good deal of information on the Resistance also emerged from the war crimes trials in Nuremberg, particularly from the first trial of the major war criminals.‡ Since then, Dulles's papers have become available at Princeton, and a great number of OSS records are now available for inspection in the National Archives at College Park, Maryland, and in the Franklin D. Roosevelt Library at Hyde Park, New York. There are also relevant records in the German Federal Archives and in the Central Archive of the Federal Security Service of Russia in Moscow.

The importance of Dulles's account, which was first published in 1947, lies partly in the information it contains *beyond* these sources. Dulles was able to use the accounts published in the two years since the war, the material from the Nuremberg trials, some unpublished accounts such as those of Albrecht von Kessel in the German Foreign Service, and of Freya von Moltke, the widow of Helmuth von Moltke, who was hanged

---

* Dulles, *Germany's Underground*, pp. XIII, 198.

† Ulrich von Hassell, *Vom andern Deutschland. Aus den nachgelassenen Tagebüchern 1938–1944* (Zurich: Atlantis Verlag, 1946); Hans Bernd Gisevius, *Bis zum bittern Ende*, 2 vols. (Zurich: Fretz % Wasmuth Verlag, 1946); Fabian v[on] Schlabrendorff, *Offiziere gegen Hitler* (Zurich: Europa Verlag, 1946).

‡ Trial of the Major War Criminals before the International Military Tribunal. Nuremberg, November 14, 1945–October 1, 1946, 42 vols., Nuremberg: Secretariat of the Tribunal, 1947–1949.

for his part in the Resistance, as well as material from Secret-State police (Gestapo) and "People's Court" files. For many years, Dulles's book was the main primary source for certain aspects of the Resistance. It contains an account by Jacob Wallenberg of his encounters with Carl Goerdeler, the civilian leader of the conspiracy against Hitler. It revealed details of the activities of the Prussian Minister of Finance, Johannes Popitz, who was hanged by the "People's Court," and his role as intermediary for Heinrich Himmler's half-hearted steps toward overthrowing Hitler after the Stalingrad catastrophe of January 1943—provided he could strike a deal for himself with the Allies. Himmler had contacted the Resistance in Germany first through SS-General Kurt Wolff in May 1943 to see whether they would support his bid to remove Hitler and to assume power himself.* Dulles learned of Himmler's thoughts from Prince Maximilian zu Hohenlohe in April 1943.[†]

A comparison of the cables—available at the National Archives in College Park, Maryland—which Dulles sent to OSS Headquarters reporting on the Resistance to Hitler in Germany, with the comprehensive historical record that scholars have been able to assemble, reveals that Dulles while in Berne was by no means fully informed on the conspiracy against Hitler. Contemporary observation is of necessity more limited than the evidence assembled years later from all available sources by

* Albert Speer, Einnerungen, Propyläen Verlag: Berlin, 1969, p. 390; Ivar Anderson, diary, October 30, 1943, Ivar Anderson Papers L 91:3, Royal Library, Stockholm; Gerhard Ritter, Carl Goerdeler und die deutsche Widerstandsbewegung, Deutsche Verlags-Anstalt: Stuttgart, 1956, pp. 360–362; Walter Schellenberg, Testimony, Nuremberg, November 13, 1945, pp. 13–19, Staatsarchiv Nuremberg NG 4718; Hassell, p. 279; Spiegelbild einer Verschwörung. Die Kaltenbrunner-Berichte an Bormann und Hitler über das Attentat vom 20. July 1944. Geheime Dokumente aus dem ehemaligen Reichssicherheitshauptamt, Seewald Verlag: Stuttgart, 1961, p. 351; T[heodor] E[schenburg], ed., "Die Rede Himmlers vor den Gauleitern am 3. August 1944," Vierteljahrshefte für Zeitgeschichte 1 (1953), pp. 375–376; Himmler's appointment diary August 26, 1943, National Archives Microcopy T–84 roll R25; [Walther Huppenkothen], Interrogation Report of Huppenkothen, Headquarters Counter Intelligence Corps United States Forces, European Theater, [1945]; OSS Research and Analysis Branch Summaries 41507S, National Archives, RG 226.

[†] Petersen, pp. 55, 154–155, 571, 586.

dozens of researchers who could take the time they needed, and who could bring together sources that had not been available to the contemporary observer.* In this case, however, there was an added impediment to a full revelation: Dulles was reporting on a conspiracy in progress. It is the nature of conspiracies that they are carried on in secrecy. At the same time, the conspirators felt they must disregard the dangers inherent to informing outsiders, namely the Allied leaders whom they hoped to find sympathetic to their cause, since the conspirators required assurances concerning the treatment of Germany after the end of the war. Many of them could not bring themselves to deliver Germany to another vindictive "Versailles" (although some were radical enough to disregard this) and to accept again, as the Republic of Weimar had, the onus of having presided over and accepted Germany's defeat, which had discredited the Republic and led to the rise of Hitler. The conspiracy needed internal support from high government officials and military leaders to succeed in its immediate aim, the overthrow of Hitler, and to survive politically long enough to establish peace. These facts as much as Dulles's skill as a spymaster enabled him to "penetrate" the German Resistance, which makes his account a document of such great value.

The importance of this account, therefore, lies above all in the validation of other accounts by an intimate expert on the Allied side. While the authenticity of sources such as Hassell's diary could hardly be questioned, Gisevius and Schlabrendorff, for different reasons, presented more pleading and less reliable accounts. Gisevius in particular colored his version with personal views and second-hand tales.

Dulles favored an interpretation of the Allied demand for Germany's "unconditional surrender" that excluded dismemberment, poverty, humiliation, and Soviet domination. While he served in Berne, he sought unsuccessfully to influence American policy in this direction. He did not argue explicitly against "un-

* See Peter Hoffmann, *The History of the German Resistance 1933–1945*, Third English Edition (Montreal, Kingston, London, Buffalo: McGill-Queen's University Press, 1996).

conditional surrender"; there was no doubt in his mind that Germany had to be defeated totally. But he believed that the Allied insistence on simultaneous surrender on all fronts unnecessarily prolonged the war. Indeed, neither his substantial espionage successes nor his memoranda on Allied policy had any measurable impact on the formulation of larger scale policy or of strategy.* Dulles believed that American policy must at least give the Germans hope for the future, and, if possible, encouragement to remove Hitler.

Gisevius, who served as an Abwehr agent in the German consulate in Zurich, argued for an arrangement between a German resistance government and the Western allies to keep the Soviet Union out of Europe, and to prevent cooperation between Hitler's successors and the Soviet Union. It was necessary, he informed Dulles in July 1944, to offer the Resistance an alternative, a vision of a new Europe in which all nations—including Germany—could exist freely and in peace rather than make demands on the men of the Resistance "which originated in the arsenal of anti-Hitler propaganda."†

Only a few in the American general staff intelligence and operations divisions, such as Colonel Vorys H. Connor and General J. E. Hull, opposed the policy of "unconditional surrender" and wanted to support the conspiracy around General Beck.‡ They wanted Germany to retain enough strength to serve as a counterbalance to Russia, and they wanted to block a Russian advance to the Mediterranean. Dulles himself advocated a sym-

---

* Petersen, pp. 9, 17.
† H[ans] B[ernd] G[isevius], memorandum for A[llen] W[elsh] D[ulles], July 1944, typescript in the author's possession; Hans Bernd Gisevius, To the Bitter End (Boston and Cambridge, Massachusetts, 1947), p. 493.
‡ Colonel Truman Smith to Allen Dulles, April 25, 1947, Allen W. Dulles Papers, Princeton University Library; Smith names Colonel Vorys H. Connor Chief of the Mediterranean Division of Operations in the Pentagon at the time, and General J. E. Hull Connor's superior in the Operations Division who, for a time, supported Connor's view; Albert C. Wedemeyer, Wedemeyer reports (New York, 1958), p. 238; on the Second Front, see Churchill, second world war 4, pp. 267–271 and passim.

pathetic hearing for the German underground,* but none of these advocates ever gained influence on American policy.

Dulles believed that assuring the German and German-occupied peoples that America intended to prevent the Soviet Union from "imposing their brand of domination on Europe," would keep these peoples from turning to the Soviets. He had urged his government in a dispatch on December 6, 1942, soon after his arrival in Berne, to put in place the necessary policies.† Gisevius took the same position and sought to convince Dulles that America must defeat not only Nazi Germany but the Bolsheviks as well, and that America needed to conclude a separate peace with Germany after the Resistance had overthrown Hitler. Gisevius, in a memorandum left behind for Dulles in Zurich when the former traveled to Berlin on July 11, 1944, advocated on the same grounds as Dulles an arrangement to have western Germany occupied by the Western powers, claiming that many Germans believed an arrangement with Russia was possible if Germany accepted a Bolshevik government.‡

After Gisevius had escaped to Switzerland in January 1945, he apparently expanded these warnings, which are reflected in Dulles's cables to Washington in January and February 1945, in which Dulles sought to induce his government to offer terms to German military leaders who surrendered in one or all of the western theaters of war. Dulles was already pursuing a secret contact with the German Supreme Commander West, Field-marshal Gerd von Rundstedt, and he had established a contact

---

* Dulles, passim; Dulles's cables from Berne in National Archives, Washington, Record Group 226 and in FDR Library, PSF box 170 and 171; cf. Arthur Bryant, *Triumph in the West, 1943–1946*: based on the diaries and autobiographical notes of Field Marshal The Viscount Alanbrooke, KG., O. M. (London, 1959), p. 242: in the interest of the balance of power, General Sir Alan Brooke suggested converting Germany to an ally against a future Russian threat rather than dismembering her.

† Allen Welsh Dulles, *From Hitler's Doorstep: The Wartime Intelligence Reports of Allen Dulles, 1942–1945*, ed. Neal H. Petersen (University Park, Pennsylvania: Pennsylvania State University Press, 1996), p. 25.

‡ H[ans] B[ernd] G[isevius], Memorandum for A[llen] W[elsh] D[ulles], typed, n.p., July 1944, Mary Bancroft papers.

with the German Supreme Commander Southwest, Fieldmarshal Albert Kesselring, in Italy.[*]

According to the editor of a selection of Dulles's wartime intelligence reports, Neal H. Petersen, "OSS Bern's coverage of the Holocaust was inexplicably meagre."[†] Allen Dulles was deeply shocked and concerned by the persecution of the Jews from 1933 onward and quarrelled with his brother about Sullivan & Cromwell's further operations in Germany. In 1942 he proposed a "tribunal" of distinguished jurists to examine all evidence about German, Italian, and Japanese perpetrators of violence.[‡] Dulles did receive information on the Holocaust from one of the most important sources on the subject, the German businessman Eduard Schulte.[§] But Petersen reprints only two reports from Dulles's war years in Berne dated March 10 and December 30, 1943 which "contributed to Washington's knowledge" about the Holocaust of March 10, 1943 and December 30, 1943, and four reports dated June 12 and July 8, 1943, and January 27 and May 31, 1944 in which he referred to the Holocaust.[‖]

Petersen states that Dulles's "reticence on this subject was among the most controversial and least understandable aspects of his performance in Bern." He speculates that Dulles chose "not to emphasize the Holocaust in his reports to Washington" because "perhaps he believed that in view of German and European anti-Semitism, highest priority denunciation of the Holocaust would be counterproductive for the purposes of Western psychological warfare," or "perhaps he feared that the

[*] *Foreign Relations of the United States. Diplomatic Papers. The Conferences at Malta and Yalta 1945*, United States Government Printing Office, Washington, 1955, p. 957; Dulles to Donovan No. 4077, January 25, 1945, OSS records, National Archives, Washington, D.C.

[†] Petersen, p. 50.

[‡] Richard Breitman, *Official Secrets: What the Nazis Planned, What the British and Americans Knew* (Hill and Wang: New York, 1998), p. 131.

[§] Walter Laqueur and Richard Breitman, *Breaking the Silence*.

[‖] Petersen, pp. 50–51, 187–188, 71, 79, 204, 296.

flight of new refugees to Switzerland would interfere with his espionage activities."* The true explanation may be less complicated. In view of the extensive information that Allied authorities in Switzerland—particularly the Berne Legation and the Geneva Consulate—received from many sources about the extermination of the Jews and in view of the great amount of information that reached the American government, but which it refused to believe or to act on until the establishment of the War Refugee Board on January 26, 1944,† it is likely that the paucity of Allen Dulles's reporting on the Holocaust reflected more the interests of his superiors than his own.

Final assessment, however, must be deferred until a great number of classified OSS records are opened. There may well be among them reports from Allen Dulles dealing with the Holocaust.

Peter Hoffmann

---

* Petersen, p. 570; see also p. 601.
† Breitman, p. 229 and passim; Petersen, p. 601.

GERMANY'S UNDERGROUND

1. Hitler's Headquarters in East Prussia, July 20, 1944

About midnight, Central European Time, July 20, 1944, Europe was startled by a radio address by Adolf Hitler. He had been silent for months. The military situation had left little for him to say. The Allied landing in France had succeeded, and the breakthrough into the interior was under way. The Russians were at the gates of Warsaw and threatening East Prussia.

"If I address you today," the Führer said, "I am doing so for two reasons. First, so that you shall hear my voice and know that I personally am unhurt and well; and second, so that you shall hear the details about a crime that has no equal in German history."

Then he described the crime:

"An extremely small clique of ambitious, unscrupulous, and at the same time foolish, criminally stupid officers hatched a plot to remove me and, together with me, virtually to exterminate the staff of the German High Command. The bomb that was placed by Colonel Count von Stauffenberg exploded two meters away from me on my right side. It wounded very seriously a number of my dear collaborators. One of them has died. I personally am entirely unhurt apart from negligible grazes, bruises, or burns."

The plot, Hitler asserted, resembled the Badoglio coup against Mussolini. The group perpetrating it "believed it could thrust a dagger into our back as it did in 1918."

Hitler naturally tried to minimize the plot's importance:

"The circle that comprises these usurpers is extremely small. It has nothing to do with the German armed forces. . . .

"It is a very small clique of criminal elements, that will now be exterminated mercilessly.

"This time," he continued, "we will settle accounts in such a manner as we National Socialists are wont." And then, shouting in typical Hitlerian style, he adjured his followers to "counter these elements at once with ruthless determination and either arrest them at once or—should they offer resistance anywhere—wipe them out."

In conclusion, the Führer proclaimed the outcome of the plot to be "a clear sign of Providence that I am to carry on with my work." And he did carry on to the bitter end.

When Colonel Count Claus Schenk von Stauffenberg left Berlin for Hitler's secret headquarters in East Prussia on the morning of July 20, he carried with him detailed plans for creating several new front-line divisions out of the Replacement Army (Ersatzheer) by scraping the bottom of the German man-power barrel. But the bulge in his briefcase was not due solely to these plans and papers. It concealed a bomb, of a kind made in England and smuggled into German-occupied countries for the use of saboteurs. The compactness and ingenious construction of these bombs had proved so interesting to the German police that they had turned them over for study to the Abwehr, the German intelligence and counterintelligence service. The bombs had no telltale clock mechanism. They were exploded by causing a glass capsule containing acid to break in a chamber in which was fixed a taut wire that held the firing pin back from the percussion cap that would set off the explosive material. The wire's thickness determined the time required for the acid to eat through the wire and release the firing pin. Several of these bombs had been set aside some time before by Stauffen-

berg's confederates in the Abwehr and stored at Berchtesgaden with General Helmuth Stieff, one of the plotters. For
it had been planned to make the attempt on Hitler's life
in his mountain retreat. When Hitler moved to his East
Prussia headquarters the bombs were taken from Berchtesgaden and delivered to Stauffenberg in Berlin.

Stauffenberg had tried twice before to assassinate Hitler.
On July 11 he had flown to Berchtesgaden; but he did not
place the bomb, because neither Himmler nor Göring was
present, and it was the desire of the plotters to kill them as
well as Hitler. Several of the highest army officers, notably
Field Marshals von Kluge and Rommel, had agreed to go
along with the plot only if both Göring and Himmler were
assassinated at the same time as Hitler.

The second attempt was to be made on July 16, when
another meeting was called at Hitler's headquarters. Again
the plan miscarried. At the last moment Hitler did not at-
tend the conference, nor did Himmler and Göring.

Stauffenberg's failures were severely criticized by his fellow
conspirators. On July 16, counting on the success of the coup,
troops in the neighborhood of Berlin, under the command
of members of the conspiracy, had been alerted to move on
Berlin. It had been difficult to find an innocent excuse for
this alert, but the officers did manage to pass it off as a practice maneuver in home defense.

The nerves of the conspirators were now strained to the
breaking point, for there was grave danger of a leak and they
were not sure that Himmler did not know of their plot. In
fact, some months earlier Himmler had told Admiral Wilhelm Canaris, chief of the Abwehr, who unknown to Himmler was privy to the conspiracy, that he, Himmler, knew a
considerable number of officers were toying with the idea
of an uprising. Himmler indicated he was so fully informed
about them he could afford to await the most favorable moment to arrest them. He had even mentioned the names of

3

two ringleaders—General Ludwig Beck and Carl Friedrich Goerdeler. On July 17 one of Himmler's chief criminologists, Arthur Nebe,* who was in the conspiracy, reported that a warrant was to be issued for the arrest of Goerdeler and that he must go into hiding at once. He did so. Julius Leber, one of the leading Social Democrats in the conspiracy, had already been arrested. About the same time a naval officer in the Abwehr, who was aware of the plans for the plot, attended a party given by one of the social leaders of Potsdam, Frau von Bredow, granddaughter of Bismarck, whose personality was so vigorous she was called "the only male descendant" of the Iron Chancellor. There the naval officer, to his astonishment, heard a young fellow officer say quite openly that an attempt on Hitler's life was being planned.

It was obvious there was no time to lose if the conspirators were to strike before Himmler did.

Stauffenberg had been chosen to place the bomb because he was the only member of the inner circle of conspirators who, without danger of being searched, had ready access to Hitler. As liaison between the commanders of the Replacement Army and Hitler's headquarters, his presence was required at some of the High Command's staff meetings, which Hitler generally attended.

The choice was somewhat unfortunate, for Stauffenberg had been severely wounded in Africa. His left arm and two fingers of his right hand were missing and the sight of his left eye was impaired. He was unable to shoot if necessary, or to do anything but set the detonator and place the bomb. But

---

* Arthur Nebe was a criminal expert in the German government when Hitler came to power. He was also a Nazi party member and became the head of the Criminal Police Department (Bureau I of Himmler's Central Security Office—the Reichssicherheitshauptamt). In 1933 Göring ordered him to do away with Gregor Strasser, one of Hitler's old comrades and the "Trotsky" of the Nazi party. An automobile or hunting accident was suggested. Nebe refused. What finally turned him against the party was the practice of issuing *blank* "murder orders" for the convenience of the Gestapo. He remained in Himmler's organization at the request of the anti-Nazis. A price of 50,000 Reichsmarks was put on his head after July 20, and he was caught and executed.

there was no question of his personal courage. He had offered to remain in the room when the bomb exploded if that were desirable. His associates vetoed such a sacrifice on the ground that he was too able an organizer to be expended in this way. Further, since Stauffenberg had helped prepare the plans for the use of the Replacement Army, he knew the units that could be counted upon by the conspirators and the reliability of their various officers. Above all, his personal popularity among his subordinates and his ability to assume an important command in the army, made Stauffenberg indispensable to the success of the putsch. He was often described as the "manager of the conspiracy."

The conspirators had several confederates at Hitler's headquarters in East Prussia. Chief among them was General Erich Fellgiebel, who was in charge of the army's Signal Corps. His task was to inform the conspirators in Berlin as soon as the bomb had exploded and then to wreck the communications center at headquarters and thus interrupt all telephone, radio, and teletype connection with the outside world. Thereby the conspirators would have time to get control of the governmental apparatus in Berlin before anyone in Hitler's entourage could set countermeasures in motion.

After the second failure, of July 16, Stauffenberg determined that on the next opportunity no matter what happened or who was present, he would place the bomb if Hitler were there. But even General Beck, the head of the conspiracy, was skeptical. "A horse that refuses a jump twice," he said, "is not likely to go over a third time." However, everyone realized these particular conspirators would never have a fourth opportunity.

Stauffenberg's chance came on July 20. Hitler had left Berchtesgaden for the east front, and his headquarters, near Rastenburg, were deep in a pine forest near one of the innumerable lakes which dot that part of East Prussia. It bore the code name "Wolfschanze," i.e., wolf's fort.

The day was hot, and the conference was shifted from one of the well protected concrete bombproof shelters, in which a bomb would have maximum effect upon human beings, to a flimsy wooden barracks. Neither Himmler nor Göring attended. As a matter of fact, Göring's advice had not been sought on military matters for some time. But the usual yes-men who surrounded Hitler were there, including Field Marshal Wilhelm Keitel and General Alfred Jodl. General Karl Bodenschatz, who was attached to Göring's headquarters some forty miles away, had arrived at Wolfschanze a few minutes before the meeting began in order to prepare the Führer for discussions with Mussolini and Graziani, who were to arrive that afternoon. When Bodenschatz finished his report Hitler asked him, according to Bodenschatz's later testimony, to come along to the usual noon briefing. "I didn't want to go," said Bodenschatz, "but I went, and fifteen minutes later the attempt at assassination occurred."

The only circumstantial and detailed account of what took place during these few crucial minutes has been given by Heinz Buchholz, one of Hitler's confidential secretaries, who was taking notes of the meeting. Here is the essence of what Buchholz told American interrogators at Nürnberg:

The July 20 briefing of the Führer was held at the usual time, 12 : 30 P.M. It began punctually with a statement by Lieutenant General Heusinger about the situation on the eastern front. Field Marshal Keitel, a few minutes late, arrived about 12 : 35, accompanied by several officers—among them Colonel Count Claus von Stauffenberg. "I remember Count von Stauffenberg," said Buchholz, "as a tall, slender man, dark-haired and dark-complexioned. He had driven over a mine during the African campaign and had been seriously injured. One of his arms was amputated, and on the day of the bomb attempt he wore a black patch over one of his eyes."

Stauffenberg had not been a frequent participant at these

6

briefings, and Hitler did not recognize him. Keitel introduced him to the Führer and stepped up to the table at the Führer's left. Stauffenberg placed his briefcase under the map table, around which everyone was standing, scarcely six feet to the right of Adolf Hitler, then moved somewhat into the background. An operations officer on the General Staff, Colonel Brandt, standing near the briefcase, found that it was in the way of his feet and moved it slightly to the right and farther away from Hitler. As a result, one of the table supports was directly between Hitler and the briefcase.

Stauffenberg, however, was unaware of this fact because, a moment earlier, at about 12 : 40, he had been called to the telephone. It was later proved by the switchboard operator that Stauffenberg's adjutant, Lieutenant Werner von Haeften, had called him to give him an excuse to get out of the room. Only a few minutes after he went out the bomb exploded. "I remember it as thunder connected with a bright yellow flame and thick smoke," Buchholz recounted. "Glass and wood splinters shot through the air. The large table on which all the situation maps were spread and around which the participants were standing—only the stenographers were sitting—collapsed. After a few seconds of silence, I heard a voice, probably Field Marshal Keitel's, saying, 'Where is the Führer?' "

Supported by Keitel, Hitler was able to walk from the barracks to his quarters. After him staggered the others, injured, bleeding, hands and faces blackened and burned, hair singed and yellowed, uniforms torn and stained.

Most of those present, including the Führer himself, at first supposed the bomb had been thrown into the room from the outside, as the windows were open, or that it had been planted under the floor. But this second hypothesis was quickly eliminated because the floor boards had been pressed down and not blown up by the explosion. The investigations, concluded that same afternoon, left little doubt that the explosive had been brought into the conference room in Stauffenberg's briefcase.

When the bomb exploded Hitler was leaning over the maps, his right arm resting on the table. This arm was partly paralyzed, and his right leg was burned and injured. Both eardrums were damaged, and his hearing was affected. Though not critically wounded, he never fully recovered from the physical and mental shocks.

A score of officers were injured and later received from their Führer a special decoration inscribed: "Hitler—July 20, 1944." Four were killed: Major General Schmundt, Chief Wehrmacht Adjutant to the Führer, who kept his military diary; General Korten; Colonel Brandt; and Heinrich Berger, one of the stenographers. Berger has often been referred to as Hitler's "double" because of a rather close physical resemblance, but there is no evidence that he was ever used to impersonate the Führer.

Meanwhile Stauffenberg had passed the guards unchallenged and reached the automobile assigned to him. There, in the parking lot, a few hundred yards from Hitler's barrack, he waited. General Fellgiebel, the chief representative of the conspiracy at the East Prussia headquarters, joined him. Together they counted off the minutes before the explosion. Then, confident that Hitler was dead, that his own work was done, Stauffenberg drove to the airfield, some fifteen minutes away, where a courier plane was waiting to fly him back to Berlin.

At this point one of the critical, and for the plotters fatal, mistakes occurred. General Fellgiebel did not blow up the communication center. Whether he lost his nerve when he saw Hitler still alive or there was some technical failure down the line will never be known. He was executed shortly thereafter, and his secret died with him. In any event, Fellgiebel's failure enabled Hitler's aides to communicate with the outside world, and, even more important, to learn what was going on in Berlin.

The Führer's first idea was to conceal the attempt at assassination from the German people. It was twelve hours later, in fact well on into the night, that he made his broadcast. By that time proof had reached the Rastenburg headquarters that Stauffenberg's bomb was not an isolated incident. Orders were being issued from the conspirators' Berlin headquarters. Berlin, Paris, Vienna, Prague, Belgrade, and many other parts of Germany and of German-occupied countries were in ferment. Frantic inquiries were pouring in to Hitler's headquarters. The Führer's voice, over the undamaged communication facilities, was a vital weapon in quelling the rebellion and in bringing the timid and faltering back into line.

By a strange coincidence Hitler had granted Mussolini, who had long been importuning him, an interview for that very day. A few hours after the attack, Hitler, with his right arm bound up, met Mussolini and Graziani at their train. They had been accompanied from northern Italy by an SS officer, Sturmbannführer Eugen Dollmann, who can best be described as a kind of diplomatic envoy in Italy of the SS (originally a Nazi elite guard and later practically a state within a state), and SS liaison with Mussolini. Dollmann has given a vivid description of the macabre meeting between Il Duce, then almost an outcast in his own country, and the Führer, who had so narrowly escaped assassination. How different from those meetings at Salzburg, Venice, and the Brenner, when the two dictators were dividing up Europe!

Hitler's inner circle, according to Dollmann, had now reached his side. Ribbentrop, who had a headquarters nearby, had arrived; so had Himmler and Göring. They were not a gay party. Hitler, still white, told Mussolini he had just had the greatest piece of luck in his life. Together they inspected the mass of debris at the scene of the explosion. At five o'clock they started their conference. The Führer was silent and for a long time sat gazing into space, munching the vari-colored pills supplied him by Professor Theo Morell, the quack he made his physician.* But the others, more or less ignoring their Italian visitors, began to quarrel, and to blame one another because the war had not yet been won. Ribbentrop raged against the generals and insisted on being called *von* Ribbentrop. (Only adoption in 1925 by his spinster aunt, Gertrud, had given him the right to use *von*.) Göring threatened him with his marshal's baton. Keitel tried to make excuses. Mussolini was aghast, and tried to maintain his dignity among the barbarians of the north.

In some way, Dollmann was not sure how or by whom, the blood purge of June 30, 1934, when Röhm was assassinated, was mentioned. That roused Hitler from his lethargy. He leaped up, and, with foam on his lips, shouted at the top of his voice that Providence had shown him once more that he was chosen to shape world destiny. He would take his revenge even on women and children! It was an eye for an eye and a tooth for a tooth if anyone set himself up against divine Providence.

This went on for half an hour, according to the SS officer, until Mussolini became quite shaken. Then footmen, in white uniforms, came in to serve tea, and Hitler calmed down. Field Marshal Graziani made an effort to change the subject and started talking to Keitel about the Italian anti-

* Hitler had unbounded confidence in Morell, who gave him special injections and pills with "pick-up" qualities. His medical advice to the Führer helped to contribute to Hitler's physical decline during the latter months of the war. During a conversation which Hitler had with Mussolini on April 23, 1944, the Führer described Professor Morell as "the best and most modern surgeon," who "had developed his own theory of bacteria of which the universities at present had only a slight knowledge." Hitler recognized the suspicion in which Morell was held by the German medical profession and compared their opposition to him to that shown in the earlier days of German medicine to Koch, remarking to Mussolini that you cannot expect that a university professor would "suddenly admit that his whole previous knowledge had become obsolete."

aircraft units which the Germans demanded for the slaughterhouse of the East.

At this point someone telephoned from Berlin to say that order had not yet been restored there. Hitler took the telephone himself and again began to shriek. He gave the SS in Berlin full power to shoot anyone they wished and completely lost his temper when he heard that Himmler, who had only just left East Prussia to take over in Berlin, had not yet arrived there.

Then Hitler calmed down, and started a monologue of self-pity. The German people, he said, were unworthy of his greatness, and no one appreciated what he had done for them. This elicited emphatic denials from his henchmen, who vied with one another to convince the Führer of their loyalty. Göring recounted what he had done for the Nazi cause and the air force. Dönitz extolled the heroism of the navy. But then Göring and Ribbentrop started quarreling again. And so it went until the SS officer led the bewildered Italian visitors away.

While this mad tea party went on in East Prussia, in the rest of Germany the blood purge began. Thousands were rounded up, arrested, tortured, and killed, in order that Hitler's Thousand Year Reich might survive another two hundred and ninety days.

2. The Evolution of a Police State

The attempt of July 20 was the culmination of a series of plots and conspiracies that began before the war. It was not an isolated, spontaneous coup, but part of a planned, desperate, last effort to destroy the Nazi tyranny. The Germans in the plot had been working secretly for years.

The German underground had its moments of high drama and of bitter frustration, its brave characters, and its pragmatic schemers. To understand this drama correctly, it is necessary to comprehend the background of Hitler's Germany against which the actors in the tragedy played their roles, and to understand how Hitler gained control of Germany and molded it into a police state.

Throughout the decade before Hitler came to power, the National Socialist German Workers Party (NSDAP) appealed to both the nationalists on the right and the workers on the left. It also gathered in elements of the population that lacked sufficient interest to vote or had no definite party affiliations—many youths as they came of voting age, and disillusioned veterans of the First World War. Hitler also profited from the world-wide depression which set in after 1929. But in the elections of November, 1932, the Nazi party's voting strength, for the first time, declined. Many Germans who had viewed its uninterrupted progress with growing alarm felt that at last the tide was receding, the danger was over. But in those same elections the Communist

12

party gained as much as the Nazis lost. Old and decrepit President Hindenburg, influenced by reactionary advisers—especially his son Oskar and his favorite Papen—was persuaded that the choice lay between Communism and Fascism, that with one more election the Communists would be in power. In a panic, he made Hitler Chancellor. This was done in such a constitutional and, to the Germans, orderly manner, that the majority in Germany failed to realize the significance of what was happening.

Many German industrialists, equally fearful of Communism, shared the view of the conservatives who helped Hitler into power and gave the Nazi party financial backing.

Dr. Hjalmar Schacht, testifying at Nürnberg, was quite precise on this point. In February of 1933, just after Hitler came to power and just before the elections that enabled him to keep it, Schacht attended at Göring's home what he described as a "financial meeting." Here is the testimony of Schacht, who mistakenly considered himself to be smarter than Hitler:

SCHACHT: Hitler had fixed the election for the 5th of March, if you will remember, and for these elections he wanted me to do the campaigning. He asked me to procure the money and I did so. Göring called these men together and I made a speech—not a speech, for Hitler made the speech—but I asked them to write down the amounts and to subscribe for the elections, which they did. They subscribed the amount of 3,000,000 Reichsmarks altogether, and they apportioned the amounts among themselves.

QUESTION: Who were the people who made up that subscription list?

SCHACHT: I think that all of them were bankers and industrialists, chemical industrialists, iron industries, textile industries, all of that. . . .

QUESTION: Do you recall any specific names?

SCHACHT: The old gentleman Krupp was there, Gustav, I think it was. Schnitzler, I think it was, was there, and Vögler for the United Steel Works.

Dr. Schacht also testified that at this same meeting Göring remarked that the sacrifice asked for—namely, the contributions to the Nazi party fund—"would be so much easier for the German people to bear if they realized that the election of March 5 [1933] would surely be the last one for the next ten years, possibly even for the next hundred years." Even brazen statements of this kind did not awaken the Ruhr industrialists to the fate in store for them. They were not interested in elections or democracy. After all, they reasoned, Hitler, like Mussolini, would give his country the "order" which the Germans so highly prized.

Hitler then proceeded to destroy his opponents, playing them off against one another, and to wreck the institutions on which liberty and democratic government are based. At the outset he pleased the nationalists by his unconstitutional exclusion of the Communists from the Reichstag and his suppression of the Socialist party. Then he turned on the junkers—Hugenberg, Papen, and associates. He lured them into acquiescence by letting them keep their freedom, their property, and sometimes even their official positions, but saw to it that they were mere figureheads. He pleased the industrialists by destroying the labor unions, and then harnessed industry to the Nazi military machine. But he left the industrialists at least ostensible control of their properties.* Then followed the destruction of *all* political parties, the suppression of the freedom of the press, the cruel extermination of the Jews and the creation of one of the most ruthlessly efficient police states in history. He even attacked the churches to prevent them from becoming an instrument for the preservation of political or personal liberty.

* Later Hitler came to regret his "leniency" in dealing with the upper strata of society. Otto Meissner, who was State Secretary in the office of the Presidency from the end of World War I through World War II, quotes Hitler as saying that Lenin and Stalin had been right in annihilating the upper classes in Russia and that he, Hitler, had made a mistake in not doing likewise. After July 20, 1944. Hitler tried to correct this "mistake."

Finally Hitler turned his attention to the High Command of the German army and to those generals who had leadership potentialities. The army tried to remain immune from Nazi influence, but its independence was slowly undermined. Some generals were won over when Hitler repudiated the provision of the Versailles Treaty that restricted the size of the German army; others, who remained hostile, were ousted—simply or deviously.

As early as February of 1934, Colonel General Kurt von Hammerstein, the most liberal of all the anti-Nazi generals, had been ordered by General (later ,Field Marshal) Werner von Blomberg, the War Minister, to relinquish all his military duties. The next June General Kurt von Schleicher, the ex-Chancellor and Hitler's most dangerous rival, was murdered during the Röhm purge. Four years later General Werner von Fritsch, Commander in Chief of the army, was discredited by means of a trumped-up charge of homosexuality, and later sought death on the field of battle in Poland. And Hitler's weak and subservient War Minister, Blomberg, was forced to resign. His marriage with a prostitute furnished Göring and Himmler the pretext they were seeking in order to get rid of him.

Hitler then unified the high commands of the army, navy, and air force. By decree of February 4, 1938, he created an over-all "Supreme Command of the Armed Forces" and became, in effect, his own War Minister. He put his faithful follower, Wilhelm Keitel, in charge of the *Oberkommando der Wehrmacht* (OKW), as the new unified command was called. By bringing the newly created and Nazi-dominated air force and the less Nazified army and navy under a single command, Hitler was trying to reduce the chances of opposition to himself arising within the armed forces.

Hitler could not have accomplished all these things without the support of the German people, including, at the end, some eight million party members. Unfortunately he also found far too many supporters in England, France, the United States, and elsewhere throughout the world. The appeal of the "strong leader" was not limited to Germany.

To those who pass judgment today on prewar Germany and express, as is often done, amazement that Hitler was not eliminated by the German people themselves long before 1939, it is not invidious, nor without point, to recall that Winston Churchill, an archenemy of German nationalism and a sophisticated master of European politics, wrote in 1935 in his book *Great Contemporaries:*

> We cannot tell whether Hitler will be the man who will once again let loose upon the world another war in which civilisation will irretrievably succumb, or whether he will go down in history as the man who restored honour and peace of mind to the great Germanic nation and brought it back serene, helpful and strong, to the forefront of the European family circle.

He added that the story of Hitler's struggle

> cannot be read without admiration for the courage, the perseverance, and the vital force which enabled him to challenge, defy, conciliate, or overcome, all the authorities or resistance which barred his path.

Mr. Churchill soon found the truth and became the foremost British prophet of the Nazi danger. But his countrymen were slow to believe him. In the first White Paper published by the British Government in World War II, on September 20, 1939, the last British Ambassador to Germany, Sir Nevile Henderson, while generally castigating most features of the Nazi system, had this to say of Hitler:

> It would be idle to deny the great achievements of the man who restored to the German nation its self-respect and its disciplined orderliness. The tyrannical methods which were employed within Germany itself to obtain this result were detest-

able, but were Germany's own concern. Many of Herr Hitler's social reforms, in spite of their complete disregard of personal liberty of thought, word or deed, were on highly advanced democratic lines. The "Strength Through Joy" movement, the care for the physical fitness of the nation, and, above all, the organisation of the labour camps, an idea which Herr Hitler once told me that he had borrowed from Bulgaria, are typical examples of a benevolent dictatorship. Nor can the appeal of Nazism with its slogans so attractive to a not over-discerning youth be ignored. Much of its legislation in this respect will survive in a newer and better world, in which Germany's amazing power of organisation and the great contributions which she has made in the past to the sciences, music, literature and the higher aims of civilisation and humanity will again play a leading part.

As for the Germans themselves, it was a commonplace, just after Hitler came to power, to hear even intelligent people say: "Let him have a taste of power. Six months of it will show up his inability to run a state—the responsibilities of government will ruin the Nazis and then we Germans will be rid of them forever." Intellectuals particularly succumbed to the illusion that Hitler and his crowd were too uncouth and too ignorant to direct the complicated mechanism of government. The experiences of the last few decades should teach all future intellectuals that it does not take "culture" to rule a state.

Even today we tend to fall into the smug and dangerous habit of dismissing Hitler as a mountebank and fool, a crazy fanatic. The truth is he was one of the smartest tyrants who ever hypnotized a people. He understood his Germans thoroughly. He bemused the common man and gave hope and confidence to millions who, under the Weimar government, had seen no way to escape from their frustrations. Hitler's firsthand knowledge of these frustrations and illusions of the masses equipped him well for the task of deceiving and leading the declassed, the uprooted and the unhappy of Germany. He had learned the secret of the demagogue, which is to proffer some explanation, no matter how specious, for mass discontent, and then to promise to ameliorate it. Hitler asserted, over and over until the least literate understood him, that the plight of the German nation and the unhappiness of the individual German were the result of the Versailles Treaty, the Jews, and the Weimar Republic, i.e., democracy. To the unemployed he promised jobs, to the veterans he promised a revival of militarism (though at first it was only the pseudo militarism of the S.A.), and to the hopeless he promised a renaissance of German glory.

Under Hitler there was a feeling of resurgence, and the average middle- and working-class German, the "little man," felt he had a better chance in the world and a new self-respect. Compared to these advantages, what, after all, were the liberties he had sacrificed? So thought the average German.

Due to Germany's defeat in World War I, the effects of inflation, and the German character, Hitler's propaganda was successful. Actually it was far from giving a true picture of the situation. In the years between the wars, except for the immediate postwar armistice years 1918-1922, Germany did not experience to any marked degree greater privations and want than many other European countries. Unemployment was serious in Germany, but it was also serious elsewhere, and in Germany it never got out of control. Under the Weimar Republic the unemployed were as well cared for by unemployment insurance and food subsidies as were the unemployed in the United States and other countries. Economically, Germany was building up. She had received huge loans from the United States and had expanded her industries and trade. While the reparation policy of Versailles was perhaps harsh, or, to put it more exactly, impractical in its written terms, Germany actually paid little except out of the proceeds of foreign loans. Some parts of her former territory were separated from her, but these losses were not disastrous economically. The Polish Corridor hurt Germany's pride, but did little to impair her chances for economic reconstruction and stability.

National Socialism was in reality a revolt against the principles of civil rights and responsibilities, against enlightenment and human progress, against the achievements of the French and American revolutions. It was infected with an adolescent romanticism whose roots were in the *Wandervögel*—a movement of revolt by German bourgeois youth against the drab regimentation of family and school life. Hess was an example of this. Lacking the determination and perseverance to develop ideals of social and political progress through hard experience, too many Germans began to despair of these ideals and proceeded to tear them down. They said they believed in democracy and the good in men, but unfortunately the majority did not see what was right; therefore democracy and progress had to be imposed upon the people from above and by force. The poison of such mental confusion is still in Germany.

The German intelligentsia, with its cultural tradition, should have done far more than it did. Its misfortune was that it did not have political experience and had lost contact with the people. The intellectuals failed to realize that democracy must never be taken for granted. They did not see the vital need for coming to its defense. To the staid and aloof professors in the German universities Hitler's movement, exemplified in an incoherent book like *Mein Kampf*, was so ridiculous that they did not take it seriously. Before they knew it, many were removed, imprisoned, or, at best, forced into silence or exile.

It was under the guise of national and moral rebirth that Hitler built up his dictatorship. There is an almost unbelievable paradox here. Many Germans, and not a few foreigners, years after Hitler came to power, still believed that a system built on the vilest intrigue and unprecedented sadism was highly moral and virtuous. What impressed them was not that the Reichstag was burned, but that Nazi decrees legislated a new kind of morality—outlawed the use of lipstick, closed shady night clubs—and that the statistics showed that criminality had declined in the Third Reich. The height of hypocrisy was reached when the Nazi writers' association (the Reichsschrifttumskammer), decreed that no more than two murders were to occur in any mystery novel, so that "the low instincts are not incited."

By the time the German people realized what their "national rebirth" and "moral awakening" actually meant, one of the most ruthless police states the world has seen was firmly established. The Nazi leaders had studied the prototype of totalitarianism in Russia. Himmler was well acquainted with the works of Trotsky and the history of the Russian secret police from the days of the Czars to that of the Cheka and the GPU. He is said to have boasted he could organize a more effective instrument of terror than had been created in Russia. In this he largely succeeded. His Central Security Office—in which he combined the secret state police (the Gestapo), the criminal police, and his security service (S.D.) with branches in foreign countries—had its secret informers in every city block, village and town. No one was safe, even in his own household. "Can you imagine what it means to work as a group when you cannot use the telephone, when you are unable to post letters, when you cannot tell the names of your closest friends to your other friends for fear that one of them might be caught and might divulge the names under pressure?" So did Count Helmuth von Moltke, one of the leading anti-Nazis, in a letter smuggled out to an English friend in 1942, describe the difficulties of plotting against Hitler.

Modern technology—the radio, telephotography, the concealed dictaphone—and the most efficient methods of detection and of torture were devoted to suppressing freedom and ferreting out any who dared to oppose the Nazi dictatorship. In a police state equipped with machine guns, tear gas, tanks and aircraft, revolutions are not made by aroused masses with their bare hands.

The statements by Churchill and Henderson I have quoted, which are but typical of what many other leaders in Europe and the United States thought and said, were to some extent a reflection of the Germans' own reaction to Hitler. The fact that such statements were made by non-Germans should help explain the befuddled state of mind of the German people under the Nazis. As Hitler gained one political and diplomatic victory after another, his popularity and power increased to the point where only a very small band of Germans dared to carry on a clandestine resistance. Those who opposed openly or whose secret opposition was discovered were relegated to concentration camps, of which some seventy to eighty existed even before the war. There are no accurate statistics on the number of Germans who passed through these camps or of those who were executed, but certainly tens of thousands of Germans, of all creeds and professions, had been made political prisoners before the outbreak of the war. Thousands fled the country.

In countries the Nazis occupied the Gestapo operated with the same cruelty, but did not prevent the Resistance in France, the Lowlands and elsewhere in Europe from performing deeds of heroism and of outstanding military importance. Germany, too, after 1933, was, in a way, an occupied country, but in a very different sense than the countries just mentioned. "Occupation" by one's own government, however vicious that government may be, creates a very different popular reaction than that which springs from occupation by a foreign government. The victims of Nazi aggression fought the foreign invader, a clearly defined national enemy; but the German anti-Nazis were fighting against their own people. They were a minority opposed to something their compatriots either supported or tolerated. In fighting Hitler for idealistic reasons, they also had to fight some of the principles and ideas which gripped the German people—such as his social reforms and his attack on the "diktat" of Versailles.

Then, too, there were not the basic, ingrained love of liberty, the independence of spirit and sense of individualism in Germany that there were in the occupied countries. A people that accepts regimentation is not likely to develop the virtue of individual initiative which a popular underground movement requires. The great majority of the German people, by 1939, either supported the Nazi regime, acquiesced in it because their livelihood depended upon it, or were terrified into silence and inaction by the political police.

There are other reasons why the anti-Nazi opposition in Germany never attained anything like the form or scope of the resistance in other Hitler-dominated countries. Underground organizations in the German-occupied countries received large-scale support from powerful allies. Arms and supplies were smuggled to them, they maintained more or less organized liaison with foreign powers, or with their own governments in exile, which could give them assistance, help them organize, inform them, instruct them, render them financial aid, and last but most important, give them the hope and moral support that kept alive their faith in ultimate deliverance.

The German underground was not an organized popular movement to which such help could be extended. Before the war the West did not take too seriously the pleas of those anti-Nazi Germans who tried to enlighten it. In those days the policy of most countries was to appease the devil himself for the sake of "peace in our time." There is considerable truth in a bitter remark of the former Chancellor of the Republic, Dr. Joseph Wirth: "The Weimar Republic and those who stood by it received nothing; the others [Nazis] everything." After Hitler went to war and Western eyes were finally opened to what Hitlerism meant, no one would have anything to do with any German, whether Nazi or not. All were suspect.

3. The Key Conspirators

It is sometimes asserted that the conspiracy to assassinate Hitler began in the early years of his regime. As a practical matter, however, it was only in 1938, when it became evident that Hitler was driving his country into a general European war, that anything like concerted action was attempted. The leaders of the conspiracy were not naïve: they knew they could not succeed without the army, which at that time was skeptical of Germany's chances in a general European war. The leading conspirators were sure that if, with the aid of the General Staff, Hitler was overthrown, the German people, no matter how Nazi-indoctrinated, would approve because they would be freed from their fear of war.

As the conspiracy developed two leading figures emerged: Colonel General Ludwig Beck, Chief of Staff of the German army until the summer of 1938, and Carl Friedrich Goerdeler, a onetime mayor of Leipzig. Closely associated with them were the former German Ambassador at Rome, Ulrich von Hassell, and Johannes Popitz, the Prussian Finance Minister who had served under the Nazis and then turned against them. Among the important military conspirators were Colonel General Kurt von Hammerstein, Commander in Chief of the German army from 1930 to 1934; General (later Field Marshal) Erwin von Witzleben; General Eduard Wagner, Quartermaster General; General Georg Thomas, head of the economic division of the planning staff of the army; Major General Hans Oster, chief assistant to Admiral Canaris, head of the Abwehr; and General Friedrich Olbricht and Colonel Claus von Stauffenberg, who had key staff positions in the Replacement Army (often called the Home Army). Wilhelm Leuschner and Julius Leber were the labor leaders most prominent in the conspiracy. Finally, there was an important group of professional men, government officials, representatives of labor and the church, centered around Helmuth von Moltke and known as the Kreisau Circle.

Only *one* of all the men named above survives: General Thomas. The others were executed by the Nazis or committed suicide—except General von Hammerstein, who died a natural death. However there were several other important members of the conspiracy who escaped, and with two of these, Hans Bernd Gisevius and Fabian von Schlabrendorff, I had particularly close contact. Gisevius, who gave sensational testimony at Nürnberg against Göring, was described before that tribunal by Mr. Justice Jackson as "the one representative of democratic forces in Germany to take this stand to tell his story." Schlabrendorff, a young lawyer in uniform, participated in one of the most sensational attempts on Hitler's life.

The military leader of the conspiracy, General Beck, was not a professional soldier by family tradition. He came of Huguenot stock, the son of a Rhineland professor, and his wife was the daughter of a prominent jurist. An intellectual as much as a soldier, he sought the company of professors and writers as frequently as that of his colleagues of the General Staff.

Beck and his friend Hammerstein were two German generals who were critical of the Prussian military spirit and sincerely tried to make the Weimar Republic work. Beck had always distrusted Hitler, but for a long time believed the German people would rid themselves of their Führer. As late as the fall of 1937 he remarked: "Because of the good qualities of the German people, it can be assumed that the Nazis will go bankrupt very soon." A year later, when synagogues were burning all over Germany and a wave of terror against the helpless Jewish Germans swept the country, his attitude changed. The anti-Semitic pogroms in November, 1938, opened the eyes of others who had hoped that somehow, some day, in some way, the Nazis would be no more.

When Hitler unleashed his war of nerves against Czechoslovakia by demanding the Sudetenland as his "last territorial demand in Europe," Beck was still Chief of Staff. He knew Hitler's aggressions could have only one result: a general war that Germany could not survive. He decided to give Hitler one more warning, and forced an interview with him in the late summer of 1938, shortly before Munich. It was his last talk with the Führer. Hitler made it clear that he was not afraid of war.

Beck's close friend, General von Hammerstein, was undoubtedly the most democratic of all Reichswehr generals. Because of his desire for friendly cooperation with Russia he was called the "Red General," and the proceedings of the Moscow trials of the late thirties disclose that he was one of the contact men in Germany for the Russian generals who were accused of attempting a Trotskyist palace revolution. Hammerstein had urged a military putsch to prevent Hitler's appointment as Chancellor on January 30, 1933, but had been frustrated by Hindenburg, who accused Hammerstein of violating the tradition that German officers should have nothing to do with politics. Hindenburg told him, Hammerstein later recounted, that he, Hammerstein, should see to it that the maneuvers that year were better than those of the preceding year. *"That* is your business," said the old Field Marshal.

The "Red General" had always been unpopular with the German Right and the nationalist army officers because he believed in and tried to uphold the Weimar Constitution. But he was on excellent terms with leaders of the trade unions and the Social Democratic party, and he put Beck in touch with his friends in these circles. Many political discussions took place in Hammerstein's villa in Berlin-Zehlendorf, where Beck brought Hassell, and later, Goerdeler.

Beck and Hassell were members of the same Berlin round-table group which dined together weekly, the Wednesday Society, many of whose members became involved, fortuitously and otherwise, in the conspiracy. Founded in the mid-nineteenth century to bring together scientists and intellectuals, the Wednesday Society's membership was traditionally confined to sixteen. Beck was its only soldier member and had been admitted because of his knowledge of military history. In addition to Beck, three Wednesday Society members became active in the conspiracy: Professor Jens Peter Jessen, Prussian Finance Minister Johannes Popitz, and Hassell.

Hassell, a career diplomat, entered the German Foreign Service in 1909 at the age of 28. He climbed the diplomatic ladder in Rome, Barcelona, Copenhagen, Belgrade, and became Ambassador at Rome in 1932. He was a close friend of Sir Nevile Henderson—they had served in Belgrade together —and frequently visited William Phillips, the American Ambassador at Rome. Hassell believed a United States of Europe was the only hope for the Continent and devoted himself to promoting it. He kept a detailed diary and prudently hid it, chiefly in Switzerland.

Hassell's stay in the Embassy at Rome, in view of his antipathy to Hitler's entire philosophy, is explicable only if it is recalled that in the early years of his power Hitler turned one face to the outside world and another to the German people. For this purpose the ambassadors who had been sent out by the Weimar Republic were useful. But when Joachim von Ribbentrop went to Italy in 1937 to develop the Rome-Berlin Axis, he went over Hassel's head, aware the latter was thoroughly opposed to the idea. Hassell even warned Mussolini against Ribbentrop and against the alliance with Hitler, and openly asserted that a military pact between two such dynamic powers was bound to lead to an explosion. Ribbentrop vainly tried to win Hassell over by telling him that he, Ribbentrop, would be the next Foreign Minister. Hassell ignored him and Ribbentrop saw to it that Hassell was dismissed.

After his discharge from the diplomatic service Hassell became an executive member of the Central European Business Convention, a kind of chamber-of-commerce organization, which afforded him a cover for travel throughout Europe, even during the war. He frequently visited General von Falkenhausen, the Military Governor of Belgium, in Brussels, and Field Marshal von Witzleben who in 1940 was in Paris. He helped to keep the latter informed of developments in the plot and won the friendly cooperation of Falkenhausen. During visits to Switzerland he established contact with Swiss and British friends and made a serious effort to learn on what terms the war could be ended if the conspirators overthrew Hitler.

The Gestapo became suspicious of him, and ultimately he had to curtail his travels. He had, nevertheless, managed to keep his connection with the plot hidden, and the first evidence of it was discovered by sheerest chance. Among the papers seized by the Gestapo after July 20 were copies of pronouncements the conspirators proposed to issue when they took over the government. On one of these documents, as the story was told to me, Hassell had inserted a few words in his own handwriting. The interlineations were identified, and Hassell's fate was sealed.

The other two members of the Wednesday Society in the inner circle of conspirators were Professor Jens Peter Jessen and Johannes Popitz. Jessen was professor of political science at the Berlin University and had been a brain truster for the Nazi party between 1931 and 1933. In the early days many intellectuals, especially those who saw in the Nazi movement a chance for social reform, had been fooled by Hitler. Jessen had been shocked by the events following 1933 into resigning from all party activities and retiring to academic life. When war broke out he became a captain in the intelligence division of the army, and from this vantage point was of great use to the conspirators. He was particularly close to General Wagner, chief of the German Quartermaster Corps, who was one of the leading militay plotters.

Johannes Popitz was a bizarre combination of intellectual and Prussian bureaucrat. It was his knowledge of classical Greek culture and art, rather than the fact that he was Prussian Minister of Finance, which admitted him to the Wednesday Society. Highly gifted but unstable, he had joined the Nazi party because of frustrated ambition, and the desire to be an officeholder as long as possible. His role in the conspiracy and his fate are to be described later.

The best known of all the men in the inner circle of activists was Carl Friedrich Goerdeler. The Nazis themselves sometimes referred to the coup d'état of July 20 as the Goerdeler Putsch. Goebbels' press, because of the Nazi desire to minimize the coup's importance, printed little information about any participants other than the military men who were executed, or committed suicide, after July 20. Goerdeler, however, was an exception. A reward of one million Reichsmarks was offered for information as to his whereabouts, and on September 11, 1944, the following announcement appeared in the German press:

All the threads of the conspiracy were in the hands of Carl Friedrich Goerdeler, who was the head of the plot and destined for the position of Reichskanzler. Since 1942 he maintained contacts between the military traitors on the one hand and the political conspirators on the other. In the course of many discussions he prepared the details of the plot. From the very beginning he initiated plans for the overthrow, and outright murder, of the Führer. After the assassination he planned to establish a military dictatorship, to set up courts-martial, and to capitulate to the enemy.

Goerdeler had fled to Konradswalde, a small village in East Prussia, and there, in a little-frequented restaurant, was recognized by a woman, Helene Schwaerzel, who had once worked in the vicinity of his summer home in near-by Rauschen. Helene, a short, fat, homely spinster of forty-four, was not a Nazi party member, but she was the type of German woman for whom Hitler seemed to have a strange fascination. When arrested after Allied occupation by a German police officer—a man who had spent eight years in Buchenwald —Helene confessed she had informed the Gestapo where Goerdeler was because she had read that he was a bad criminal and she believed what her Führer told her. The million marks blood money received directly from Hitler's own hands was still unspent when the Allies arrested her.

Goerdeler was born in Schneidemühl, Prussia, in 1884 and studied law and political science at Göttingen, where he took his doctor of law degree in 1908. He became the proverbial German official—conscientious but romantic, intellectual but devoted to the state and every concept of law and order. He was a devout Protestant and a public servant par excellence. It took a Hitler to make such a man a revolutionary.

In 1930 Goerdeler became mayor of Leipzig, where the great industrial exposition was held annually and industrialists from Germany and the rest of Europe foregathered. Goerdeler made it a point to become a personal friend to these men. A year later, at the request of Chancellor Brüning, he accepted the post of Reich Commissar for Price Control. When the intrigues of General von Schleicher and Franz von Papen succeeded in overthrowing the Brüning government in 1932, Brüning suggested Goerdeler as his successor and regarded him as the man most likely to dam the tide of Nazism. Hindenburg chose Papen.

Although Goerdeler refused the appeal of Alfred Hugenberg to participate in the Nazi Rightist coalition government of 1933 which brought Hitler to power, he did serve as price commissar under Hitler from 1933 to 1936. His friends maintain he continued on in this office so he could fight Hitler and the Nazi policies from a more advantageous position. They say he tried to cross Hitler's plans for rearmament by insisting on publishing the national budget to show up the otherwise concealed increases in the national debt. He engaged in a fierce struggle with Hjalmar Schacht, whom he accused of aiding the Nazis' schemes for world domination. It is quite possible that Goerdeler's low opinion of Schacht, who was never really loyal to any cause or any person, was the reason Schacht was not taken into the inner circle of the conspiracy. His casual excursions into the field of anti-Hitler intrigue belong to a later chapter.

Goerdeler's government career ended in 1936, shortly after he had been confirmed for an additional twelve-year term as mayor of Leipzig. There had been considerable Nazi opposition to him, and he probably would not have been reappointed but for the fact that the Nazis did not wish to stir up an incident on the eve of the Olympic games in Berlin. However, Goerdeler remained mayor only a short time. The Nazi party in Leipzig had insisted upon the removal of the monument to the German Jewish composer Mendelssohn, who had spent the most important years of his life in Leipzig. Goerdeler had refused. While he was absent from Leipzig, Nazi Storm Troopers removed the monument. When Goerdeler learned of this upon his return he resigned at once. This incident may well have been the turning point in his career. From then until his death he devoted himself to plotting the overthrow of the Nazis.

In 1937 Goerdeler visited the United States and England.

He came to America to warn against Nazi intentions and to find out whether there would be any support abroad for anti-Hitler activity within Germany. He saw a number of government officials in Washington, well known public figures and leading German refugees. He tried to persuade people in this country, as well as in England, that there were anti-Nazis in Germany.

During his stay here Goerdeler wrote a political testament which was to be published only with his approval or in case of his death. He knew his days might well be numbered. This testament is an indictment of Nazi acts, policies and intentions, and ends with an analysis of the reasons why Goerdeler thought the Nazis would be compelled "to turn against the Christian faith itself, if they want to stay in power. The fight against the individual churches is only the preparation and camouflage of the real struggle. This will be against Christianity."

Despite Goerdeler's realization of the Nazi peril, he greatly overestimated the strength of the relatively feeble forces within Germany which were opposing it. Optimistic by temperament, he was often led to believe that plans were realities, that good intentions were hard facts. As a revolutionary he was possibly naïve in putting too much confidence in the ability of others to act. Like General Beck, he hoped and believed that the German people would come to their senses before it was too late. On the other hand, he was one of the few Germans with foreign contacts who saw the trend of German foreign and domestic policy and had the courage to discuss it frankly and openly.

Goerdeler has often been described as a romantic reactionary, but his great personal courage and unflinching opposition to Nazism from 1936 on have never been questioned. He often seemed reckless and indiscreet in the way he risked attracting Gestapo suspicion to himself. When a general whom Goerdeler was trying to win over resisted on the ground that it was easy for Goerdeler to incite others to actions for which he would not have to pay, Goerdeler is reported to have immediately written out in longhand and signed an indictment of the Nazis and an appeal to overthrow their regime, and to have given this paper to the general. "I want you to know," said Goerdeler, "that I am ready to take full personal responsibility for my actions and that I am willing to risk my life in this struggle." Goerdeler did so—and lost his life.

In Nazi Germany telephones were tapped, mail was censored, and every servant, taxicab driver or messenger was regarded as a possible Nazi agent. All the key conspirators used code names in conversation and correspondence. Meeting places were changed constantly. Discussions were usually held in the homes of members thought to be least suspected —those of Professor Jessen in Berlin-Dahlem, and Johannes Popitz in the same suburb, and of Dr. Sigismund Lauter, a Catholic physician, who was the head of Berlin's large St. Gertrauden Hospital. It was felt that a doctor, continually receiving patients, provided excellent cover. When General Olbricht, deputy chief of the Replacement Army, joined the conspiracy his rooms in the War Office in the Bendlerstrasse in Berlin were frequently used. No conferences were held which were not absolutely necessary.

As the conspiracy widened, the "cell" principle was employed, as in every underground movement. Each new initiate learned the names of only a few of the other conspirators. In the Third Reich the trustworthiness of even the best intentioned could never be completely relied upon, for sometimes even the bravest could not withstand the Gestapo's ways of extracting information. And not even the smallest and most insignificant cell was safe from Gestapo infiltration.

The inner circle gradually enlarged. General Beck drew in other army officers, as well as friends and former colleagues on the General Staff. Goerdeler found allies in business circles, and the Bosch plant in Stuttgart furnished him business "cover" for his travels in Germany and abroad. Hassell brought in a number of important Foreign Office officials, including Count Werner von der Schulenburg, the last German Ambassador in Moscow. Popitz enlisted Albrecht Haushofer, the son of Hitler's geopolitician and himself professor of geopolitics in Berlin. Such moderate conservatives as Baron Karl Ludwig von Guttenberg, editor of the well known Catholic *Weisse Blätter,* and Max Habermann, one-time leader of the white-collar workers union, were won over. So were some former Center Party members and other friends of Chancellor Brüning, including Paul Lejeune-Jung, Dr. Joseph Wirmer and Andreas Hermes.

The men in the inner circle were largely planners. A plot must also be executed. In Hitler's police state this required military help.

4. The Generals: Before War

The officers of the German High Command at first looked on the Nazis as rowdies, upstarts and incompetents. But just as many industrialists came to see in Hitler's demagogy a weapon against Communism, so many officers came to regard it as an antidote to the pacifist internationalism of the Left. The dynamic revolutionary character of Nazism was not taken seriously. Nevertheless, the generals did not really relish Hitler's appointment as Chancellor and they hoped the old-line conservatives who participated in the government with the Nazis —Hugenberg, Neurath, Seldte, Papen—would slowly undermine the "incapable corporal" and eventually control and then crush him.

The exact opposite occurred. With the help of his ambitious and pliable War Minister, Field Marshal Werner von Blomberg, Hitler beguiled a group of high ranking officers with promises of enormous rearmament and a revival of the privileges the officer caste had enjoyed under the Kaiser. One of the earliest and most faithful converts was General Walter von Reichenau. Other generals, like Brauchitsch, Bock, Rundstedt, Leeb and List, adopted the convenient position that the Reichswehr was "un-political." Not so General von Schleicher, who was politically minded and had tasted power during his brief period as Chancellor. He argued that the military should be the decisive influence in

German politics, and hence, logically, he was the Nazis' first important military victim.

The attitude in the early years of Nazi power of those officers whose only concern was their profession, is aptly described by General Thomas, the head of the economic branch of the German War Office, who later joined the anti-Hitler conspiracy. In a letter to his wife written in 1945 on the first anniversary of July 20, and after he was liberated from a Nazi concentration camp by the Allies, he said:

> I worked hard at my job because I realized that a disarmed Germany in the midst of highly armed nations was an impossibility and a danger to the peace. In spite of the Versailles Treaty the Western powers did not disarm—Russia armed to a large extent. Consequently something had to be done in Germany. When Hitler reintroduced conscription in the spring of 1936 the Western powers did not object. Occupation of the Rhineland had no consequences, except that England signed a naval treaty with Hitler. So every intelligent German came to the conclusion that the Western powers saw in Germany a bulwark against Bolshevism and welcomed German rearmament.

In the affidavit of Marshal von Blomberg, read to the International Tribunal at Nürnberg, the attitude of the German generals toward the Nazis after they came to power is summed up as follows:

> Before 1938-39 German generals did not oppose Hitler. There was no reason to oppose him since he produced the results they desired. After this time some generals began to condemn his methods, and lost confidence in the power of his judgment. However, they failed as a group to take any definite stand against him, although a few of them tried to do so and as a result had to pay with their lives or their positions.

The blood purge of June 30, 1934, is often explained as the liquidation within the Nazi party of those numerous innocents who took Hitler's Socialist pretensions seriously and of their principal protagonists, Röhm and Gregor Strasser. This is a partial analysis. It was also directed against the conservatives led by Papen and against the politically minded elements in the army led by General von Schleicher. The extent of the Nazi infection among the generals was clearly revealed by the 1934 purge. The most ambitious generals, particularly Blomberg and Reichenau, cooperated. The others remained tolerantly quiescent while Schleicher and his political aide, Bredow, were murdered. The generals were rewarded. Hitler permanently abandoned his attempt to create, out of the Storm Troopers of the S.A., a military rival to the Reichswehr.

A month later President von Hindenburg died and his will—about which there have been innumerable rumors—recommended that Hitler succeed him as President and continue to be Chancellor as well. Whether the will was a fake, as many assert, or was merely extracted from the ill old man (his estate had been guarded by the SS for a year and few who were not Nazis had access to him) was of no consequence in the Germany of that day. Hitler at once combined both offices in his own person, legalized the designation "Führer," and announced that every member of Germany's armed forces would have to take an oath to the person of Adolf Hitler. Shortly thereafter the Swastika, until then the symbol of the Nazi party only, not of the Reich, was sewn on the army's field-gray uniforms and became the official German flag. No one objected.

In an age as cynical as the present, we are likely to pass too casually over the significance which the German officer corps attached to an oath. In reality it was an important factor in Nazi control of the Wehrmacht. Here is a literal translation of the oath, as decreed by Hitler:

I swear by God this holy oath that I will render unconditional obedience to the Führer of the German Reich and people, Supreme Commander of the German Armed Forces, Adolf Hitler, and that as a brave soldier I will be prepared at all times to give my life for this oath.

If the German officer corps had taken this oath to their country, to its constitution, or to the German people, Hitler would not have been quite as secure as he was for as long as he was. Only a few generals rose above this primitive conception and put duty to country ahead of the oath.

General Franz Halder, who later succeeded General Beck as Chief of Staff and who time and again was on the threshold of acting on behalf of the conspiracy, explained his dilemma during the course of his interrogation at Nürnberg:

HALDER: You reproach me that in spite of my responsibility I tried to overthrow Hitler and that I was ready to overthrow him.

INTERROGATOR: Please be assured that if I were to reproach you, it would be for not overthrowing Hitler.

HALDER: May I make a personal remark? I am the last masculine member of a family who for 300 years were soldiers. What the duty of a soldier is I know. I know, too, that in the dictionary of a German soldier the terms "treason" and "plot against the state" do not exist. I was in the awful dilemma of one who had the duty of a soldier and also a duty which I considered higher. Innumerable of my old comrades were in the same dilemma. I chose the solution for the duties I esteem higher. The majority of my comrades esteemed the duty to the flag higher and more essential. You may be assured that this is the worst dilemma that a soldier may be faced with. That is what I wanted to explain.

The power of this oath, both as a compulsion to loyalty and a disguise for lethargy or fear, was manifest in even the last moments of the war. At the end of April, 1945, I was negotiating from Switzerland for the surrender of the German armies in northern Italy. Everything had been arranged—the envoy of General von Vietinghof, commander in chief of the Italian theatre, had accepted the surrender terms, which had already been signed at Field Marshal Alexander's Allied Headquarters in Caserta. All that remained was to announce the terms and put them into effect when General von Vietinghof was subordinated as Supreme Commander in Italy to Field Marshal Kesselring. Kesselring's ratification was sought in a dramatic hour-long conversation by telephone between the German headquarters in Italy and Kesselring's headquarters, then in the Austrian Tyrol. It was April 30. Minutes were vital if Alexander's surrender terms were to be met.

Hitler was reported to be dying but Kesselring, stubborn German militarist, true to his officer corps training, categorically refused to take action until he was released from his oath to the Führer by formal announcement of Hitler's death. The fact that further resistance was hopeless, that the generals in command of the Italian theater had agreed to go along, oath or no oath, had no influence on Kesselring. Fortunately, the announcement of Hitler's death came a few hours later; the situation was saved and the surrender went through. But Kesselring had stuck to his oath.

In spite of the oath, the gradual infiltration of Nazi elements into the army from 1934 on, and such diplomatic successes as rearmament, conscription and the occupation of the Rhineland, which had vastly impressed the generals, Hitler still had reason to doubt that all of the higher officers of the General Staff would follow him in a policy of European aggression. The generals, of course, knew the limitations of Germany's military potential in a world war, and they did not want such a war set off by some impetuosity of an erstwhile corporal. As General Beck told my friend Colonel Truman Smith, the American Military Attaché in Berlin in the crucial prewar days: "Hitler will be Germany's undoing. He far overestimates our military power. Sooner or later there will be a catastrophe. Can you not do something to help my poor country?"

Driven by internal exigencies, beguiled by the delusion that the concessions of an appeasing outside world were his own achievements, Hitler, in 1938, was in no mood to listen to generals who warned him against joining Austria to the Reich if doing so entailed the use of force. They had always been wrong before—and Hitler had to have Austria. The time had come to put an end to the "defeatism" of the High Command.

Both Göring and Himmler had long been intriguing to take over the War Ministry and to consolidate the Nazi control of the armed forces. As a further step in this direction they desired to get rid of Blomberg, the War Minister. He was a stupid man and had been one of the most subservient of Hitler's followers. Nevertheless he was not trusted by the fanatical Nazis, who could not forget that he was one of the reactionaries who had held over from the cabinet Hitler inherited in 1933. Also he stood in the way of their ambitions. He had to go.

An opportunity soon came. Shortly before the Nazi coup d'etat in Austria, in January 1938, Blomberg married his secretary, a commoner named Erna Gruhn. Hitler was one of the official witnesses at a formal wedding ceremony. Almost at once all Berlin knew that Erna Gruhn and her mother owned a massage parlor in a dubious section of Berlin, and that Fräulein Gruhn herself had been a prostitute. The more knowing added that very probably she had been planted in Blomberg's office by Himmler. In any event it was Himmler who brought the evidence to the attention of Hitler, and Blomberg was ousted.

The elimination of Blomberg and Fritsch, and the creation of a Nazified high command, described above, was followed by Ribbentrop replacing Neurath as Foreign Minister and Funk replacing Schacht in charge of the Reich's economy. The SS elite guards were transformed from a mere bodyguard for party leaders into a fully integrated military organization, outside the jurisdiction of the army General Staff. SS men were assigned to be political commissars and spies in regular army units, and in time became an important element in the Nazi control of the army.

The internal preparations for external aggression were thus complete. Austria was taken.

The crisis over the Sudetenland of Czechoslovakia in the summer of 1938 quickened in the members of the Beck-Goerdeler conspiracy a hope that the time to strike had come. Many General Staff officers openly expressed their fear of a two- or three-front war and in July Colonel General Wilhelm Adam, Commander in Chief of the Forces in the West, resigned in protest against Hitler's intentions to attack. The conspirators approached one general after another, this time with evidence which seemed to them conclusive, that Hitler was driving Germany inevitably into a European war.

General Beck, still Chief of Staff, decided to make his opposition to war known, and sent to the entire General Staff a memorandum proving Germany was incapable of winning a European war. The memorandum was based on a study, by high ranking generals during the winter of 1937, of the strategical possibilities for Germany in the event of a war in which Czechoslovakia and France took part. The conclusions of the study were that while initial success against the weaker opponent, Czechoslovakia, could be expected, ultimate defeat in the West was inevitable. Beck added, in his memorandum, that any armed conflict anywhere would result in a world war. According to General Halder's testimony at Nürnberg, Brauchitsch, who had succeeded Blomberg, approved the ideas contained in Beck's memorandum and himself made its contents known to a number of generals who were not on the General Staff. Hitler heard about the memorandum circulating before it reached him through official channels, and demanded to see it. When Brauchitsch took it to Hitler (in July, 1938) he warned the Führer against any steps that might lead to war. Hitler brushed the warning aside. He was interested in only one thing: Who had read the memorandum?

Working through a high official of the German Foreign Office who was a fellow conspirator, and in cooperation with Admiral Canaris and General Oster of the Abwehr, Beck informed the British of Hitler's plans and urged an unequivocal declaration by Britain that any violation of Czech neutrality would mean war. The conspirators believed that after such a statement the leaders of the German army would gain a new self-confidence and could be rallied against Hitler. When Beck's message reached the British Government, in the second week of September, the decision had already been made to send Chamberlain to see Hitler at Berchtesgaden. But Beck did not know this, and called a meeting of the chief army group commanders.

At this meeting Beck declared another world conflict to be at hand, and that it would end in a catastrophe for Germany. He said he was prepared to confront Hitler with a refusal to act against Czechoslovakia and asked his colleagues to pledge themselves to refuse to succeed him if, as was anticipated, he made no impression on Hitler and resigned. A few days later Beck had his—last—interview with the Führer. Beck told Hitler he could not assume responsibility for a military situation to which he considered the army unequal. Hitler, who already knew Beck's views (from the staff memorandum), said he would accept Beck's resignation. But in order not to affect morale in the lower echelons and in the ranks of the army, Beck's departure was kept secret for over a month.

General Halder took over Beck's duties during this period and later succeeded Beck as Chief of Staff. This deviation from the agreement with Beck was explained on the ground that Halder was to act *with* the conspirators against Hitler. The plan, briefly, was for the High Command to remove Hitler. General von Witzleben was to be in direct charge of the military forces, but the orders would be issued by the Commander in Chief of the army, General von Brauchitsch, and his Chief of Staff, General Halder. After Hitler's removal, according to Halder's interrogation by United States Army investigators at Nürnberg, Hitler was to be succeeded by a military dictatorship which Brauchitsch would temporarily head. This dictatorship was to last until the German state and people had been denazified. A complete record of Nazi crimes had been prepared by Admiral Canaris for use in educating the German people after Hitler was arrested.

But General von Brauchitsch was to be told only at the very last moment. "I had never talked to Brauchitsch expressly about this," General Halder testified. "But he knew my attitude, and he had a notion of what was going on. Once he came to see me when Witzleben was with me, and Witzleben spoke in such a way that Brauchitsch could not help but understand unless he was deaf. In case the plot did not succeed, I had to keep my Commander in Chief in the clear. I may risk my own neck, but not someone else's."

At the very last moment Halder suggested that a civilian head would be better for the post-Hitler government. Neurath was thought of, and so were Otto Gessler and Gustav Noske, who had been ministers of war during the Weimar Republic. Such a government, it may be noted, would not have had much popular appeal. Both Gessler and Noske were scorned by the militant Left and were, indeed, men of the past, incapable of understanding the problems with which any government succeeding Hitler would have to deal.

It is obvious from what Halder told American Army interrogators that though he then agreed it was necessary to remove Hitler, he was not satisfied with the conspirators' political program. He complained that none of the people who urged him into action—Goerdeler, General Beck, Admiral Canaris, General Oster and Hjalmar Schacht (who had been consulted at certain phases of the conspiracy)—had any clear-cut plan on which they had unanimously agreed. Moreover he did not trust Goerdeler's discretion, and to Schacht he said: "The people who put Hitler into power should get rid of him. . . . You elected Hitler, you put him in power. We soldiers had no right to vote." And whenever political questions were discussed, Halder would say: "I am a soldier, not a politician."

However, despite the vagueness of the political plans, Halder was, or so he says, ready to proceed, and so was General von Witzleben in Berlin. Halder agreed that the three conditions necessary for a successful *military* coup were fulfilled:

1. Resolute leadership with clearly defined responsibility.
2. The fear of war haunting the German people would make them willing to trade Hitler for peace.
3. Correct timing; Hitler's order to attack Czechoslovakia would be the signal to strike.

Hitler was expected back in Berlin, after attending the Nürnberg Party Congress, on September 14 or 15, and the conspirators were waiting to "have the bird back in its cage," as Oster put it. But a complication developed when Hitler decided to go to Berchtesgaden before returning to Berlin, and on September 14 Chamberlain announced he would visit Hitler at Berchtesgaden. The conspirators were stricken with doubt. General Beck insisted that the situation had not changed essentially, but most of the others, seeking an easy way out, argued that the fundamental premise on which they had proposed to act, i.e., that Hitler was precipitating a European war, no longer existed. Dissension among the conspirators was partially quelled when Dr. Paul Schmidt, Hitler's interpreter, sent the conspirators word that Hitler intended to propose unacceptable conditions to Chamberlain. Thereupon the probability of war revived. It was then decided that Hitler's return to Berlin would be the signal for the putsch.

After Chamberlain's second visit to Hitler war seemed certain. General Oster and Schacht asked Halder if he was still willing to act. Would he arrest Hitler? Halder shied, and advocated an assassination that could be made to appear an accident. Halder was willing to make some military dispositions that might be useful in case an "accident" should occur, and an army division, under the command of General Erich Hoeppner, was stationed in Thuringia to cut off the elite SS troops in Munich should they attempt to march to relieve Berlin. General von Witzleben, commander of the Berlin military district, was still willing, and Oster's deputy, Hans Gisevius joined Witzleben's staff to help prepare decrees and emergency edicts. From Arthur Nebe, the conspiracy's contact man in the Gestapo, came a list of the Gestapo's *secret* bases. These were marked on a map and handed to the commander of the Potsdam Division, General von Brockdorf, who was in the plot. The Abwehr reported that the British Government's vacillations had become known to the Nazis and had stiffened Hitler's attitude. The telephone line between London and Prague ran through Germany and was tapped, and the phone conversations between the Czech Legation in London and the Foreign Office in Prague were recorded.

On September 26 Hitler made the violent speech in the Sportspalast in which he promised: "The Sudetenland will be my last territorial demand in Europe." On the 27th he ordered one of his new panzer divisions to parade in Berlin to put the people in a warlike mood. But even in front of the Reich Chancellery the troops were greeted with no enthusiasm and only a few hands were raised in the Nazi salute. Hitler was furious. Goebbels toured the city in an open car to sample public opinion and reported that, mal-treated Sudeten "Volksgenossen" or no, Berliners wanted no shooting. Nevertheless, General Oster informed the conspirators that war against Czechoslovakia was about to be declared.

Early on the 28th the conspiracy's liaison in London telephoned to Berlin that he was sure any act of aggression by Hitler would mean a general war. This message reinvigorated the conspirators and the military putsch was set for the next day. Even the hesitant Brauchitsch, it was reliably reported, was willing to go along.

But around 11 o'clock on the morning of the 28th an urgent call came in to the German Foreign Office from the Italian Foreign Minister. Ribbentrop was not there, and Count Ciano asked to be put through to the Italian Ambassador, Attolico. As usual the Foreign Office listened in, and the conspirators were later informed of the following conversation between Mussolini, who was at Ciano's elbow, and the Italian Ambassador in Berlin:

MUSSOLINI: This is the Duce speaking. Can you hear me?
ATTOLICO: Yes, I hear you.
MUSSOLINI: Ask immediately for an interview with the Chancellor. Tell him the British Government asked me through Lord Perth to mediate in the Sudeten question. The point of difference is very small. Tell the Chancellor that I and Fascist Italy stand behind him. He must decide. But tell him I favor accepting the suggestion. You hear me?
ATTOLICO: Yes, I hear you.
MUSSOLINI: Hurry!

At noon Witzleben went to Halder's office to receive the orders that would start the putsch. In the midst of this crucial conversation word came that the British Prime Minister and the French Premier would meet with Hitler in Munich the following day. "Therefore I took back the order of execution," Halder said, "because the entire basis for the action had been taken away."

Halder also testified:

Now came Mr. Chamberlain and with one stroke the danger of war was avoided. Hitler returned from Munich an unbloody conqueror exalted by Mr. Chamberlain and M. Daladier. Of course the German people cheered him. Even among Hitler's opponents in the senior-officers corps his success made an enormous impression. I do not know if a non-military man can understand what it means to have the Czechoslovak army eliminated by a stroke of the pen, and Czechoslovakia, stripped of all her fortifications, standing naked like a new-born babe. With a stroke of the pen a victory was attained.

I want to emphasize once more the extreme importance which must be attributed to this Munich agreement, not only because of the impression it made on the population, but also on the Wehrmacht. From this time on you could always hear the saying: "Well, the Führer will do it somehow, he did it at Munich." May I add that Chamberlain, when he returned to London, was applauded by the people although *he* had no success to report. Adolf Hitler was even more applauded, as he had scored a success.

Some generals continued to talk about a putsch, but the opportunity was gone. Even worse, the military lost faith in the civilian conspirators, who had been sure Britain and France would not give Hitler Czechoslovakia. This faith only partly revived when General Oster learned from Keitel that the tempo of German rearmament would not be reduced because of the Munich agreement, but accelerated.

The disappointment of the conspirators is well expressed in a letter dated October 11, 1938, which Goerdeler wrote to an American friend:

The development of the past weeks can only be called very dangerous. The German people did not want war; the army was ready to do everything to prevent it. Only Hitler, Himmler and

47

Ribbentrop wanted war. Increasing inner difficulties caused them alarm. But on the other hand they told the army repeatedly that neither England nor France would be able to protect Czechoslovakia. Nobody in Germany wanted to believe them in this. But they were right. . . .

Hitler and Göring have bluffed the entire world. But the world had been warned and informed in time. If these warnings had been heeded, and if one had acted accordingly, Germany would be free of her dictator today and could turn against Mussolini. In a few weeks we could begin to shape a lasting peace which would be based on justice, reason and decency. Germany with a government of decent men would have been prepared to solve the Spanish problem together with France and England, to remove Mussolini and to create peace in the Far East in cooperation with the United States. The way might have been open for good cooperation in the economic and social fields and for pacification between labor, capital and the state, for an elevation of moral concepts, and for a new effort to raise the general standard of living. . . .

By shying from a small risk Mr. Chamberlain has made war inevitable. Both France and England will now have to defend their freedom with force of arms unless they prefer the life of slaves. However, they will have to fight under far worse conditions. . . .

But the risk was not small. Great Britain and France could not be sure that a firm stand at Munich would have brought about a revolt within Germany. Hitler was not bluffing. The opening paragraph of Hitler's secret instructions on May 30, 1938, to the High Command to prepare Operation Green, the code name for the Czechoslovak invasion, was: "It is my unalterable decision to smash Czechoslovakia by military action in the near future."

Halder was interrogated on this point:

QUESTION: Do I understand you to say that if Mr. Chamberlain had not come to Munich, your plan would have been executed, and Hitler would have been deposed?

48

HALDER: I can only say the plan would have been executed, I do not know if it would have been successful.

All that can be truly said now is that the chances of an internal revolt against Hitler were greater just before Munich than at any time thereafter until the tide of military conquest turned in 1943. The British and French can not be blamed for refusing to put much confidence in conspiratorial German generals and civilians, although in failing to have better secret liaison with them an opportunity was lost which astute diplomacy might have exploited. But their fatal mistake was handling the Sudeten crisis without Russia. In the fall of 1938 the fear of a two-front war dominated the German General Staff and made possible its participation in a putsch if convinced that Hitler's rashness would bring Russia as well as England and France against them. That they feared this is evident. The top secret staff plans for the Czech invasion, drawn up as late as August 25, 1938, contained this basic assumption: "The Soviet Union will probably side immediately with the Western powers."

Despite Munich the conspirators did not give up. In December they learned through the Abwehr channels that Hitler was planning to march into Prague and finish off Czechoslovakia. Once more the putsch apparatus was mobilized, once again Goerdeler, Hassell, Gisevius and others tried to convince the generals that this time Britain and France would really resist. Admiral Canaris and several members of his Abwehr told the generals that the civilians were right at last. Schacht advocated Hitler's immediate arrest or a coup d'état to save the peace. Finally, General Halder promised to remove Hitler *if war was declared.*

It wasn't. The occupation of all Czechoslovakia elicited only pious protestations. The conspirators were wrong once again, and the generals' respect increased for the "sleepwalker" with a "lucky star" who was always right.

Hitler's self-confidence became unbounded. In mid-August of 1939, just before his pact with Stalin was announced, he called his generals together and harangued them about the coming campaign in Poland. War had to come in his lifetime, he asserted, for: "There will probably never again be a man in the future with more authority than I have. My existence is therefore a factor of great value. But I can be eliminated at any time by a criminal or an idiot." Hence there was no time to lose. "As for our enemies," Hitler continued, "they are men below average, not men of action, not masters. They are little worms. *I saw them at Munich.*" His only fear, he told the generals, was lest "at the last minute some *schweinehund* will make a proposal for mediation."

When General Thomas, a few days before the fateful September 1, told Keitel that even with Russia neutral Germany could not win, Keitel interrupted him and declared that a world war would not occur, that the French were too pacifist and the British too decadent to aid Poland. Thomas replied that men who knew Britain and France had a different opinion and that perhaps Ribbentrop had not informed the Führer correctly. Keitel replied: "You are infected by the pacifists who refuse to see the Führer's greatness."

As September 1st and war approached the conspirators'· hopes rose again. Halder still professed to be willing to issue the decisive orders and arranged that he be informed of a declaration of war twenty-four hours in advance. Twenty-four hours, he calculated, would be ample for Hitler's arrest and the demobilization of the SS. Brauchitsch was worked on once more, and General Oster of the Abwehr told him Hitler intended to film a fake invasion of Germany by Poland with SS men and concentration camp inmates dressed in Polish uniforms and to use it as justification for Germany's invasion of Poland. Brauchitsch was again asked to try to persuade Hitler that a world war would be lost, but this was proposed to Brauchitsch more to prove to him that Hitler and the Nazis this time meant war than because of any hope Hitler would be impressed.

In addition to these attempts to influence generals, the conspirators sent several warnings to the Allies. Adam von Trott, a Foreign Office official whose prominent part in the plot is described later, talked to members of the British Government in London. Ulrich von Hassell repeatedly visited the British Ambassador in Berlin, Nevile Henderson. Fabian von Schlabrendorff, who played an important role in the 1943 attempt to assassinate Hitler, also had contact with the British. He told me that he came away with the feeling that Henderson was fascinated by the Nazis and had been immensely impressed by the party convention at Nürnberg, which to Schlabrendorff was nothing but a disgusting exhibition of mass hysteria.

On August 24, 1939 (Halder puts it on August 26), Hitler gave the order to attack Poland—without giving Halder advance notice. Three hours later he rescinded the order. The mobilization stopped, but not in time to prevent a German advance on the Jablunka Pass from Czechoslovakia into Poland. Hitler had an attack of nerves and the generals believed that the immediate crisis was past. Germany, in all its history, had never mobilized and then held back. "This means fifty years' peace," Canaris exclaimed when he heard that the attack order was rescinded. It is only recently that this reversal of the first attack order has become known. The motives of this reversal are still not clear. Possibly Hitler decided to wait a week to get the full benefit of his Russian pact, which Keitel called "the greatest act ever accomplished by a German statesman."

In those last days of peace Hitler kept himself in almost complete isolation and saw practically no one but Himmler and Ribbentrop, both of whom were urging him on to war. He did have one more conference with his generals to inform them that after Poland's conquest the population was to be treated with pitiless severity. If generals did not wish to be burdened with the political liquidations that would be necessary, Hitler graciously remarked, the Führer would not insist but would order his SS to perform the task. However, the very hope of Polish revival had to be wiped out, and this would mean the execution of thousands of aristocrats, intellectuals, and clergy. Hitler asked only that the army not interfere with the SS. None of the generals objected.

A few days later, Hitler ordered the invasion of Poland. He gave his generals twelve, not twenty-four, hours' advance notice. There was no putsch. General Halder explained that action would merely be postponed until the first defeat after the outbreak of war. Failing to appreciate that the British and French would not start the wholesale bombing of cities, the military conspirators expected that the Ruhr and Rhineland would be raided. Then the German people would realize the war was not to be "a campaign of flowers as it had been when they marched into Austria and Czechoslovakia." But there was no defeat. The Ruhr was bombarded with leaflets.

5. The Generals: During War

War did not stop the conspiracy. It merely made it more difficult, and some of the weak fell by the wayside.

General von Hammerstein, who never had to be urged to act against Hitler, had been called from retirement just before the Polish invasion and put in command of one of the German armies on the Rhine. He succeeded in arranging for Hitler to visit him at his field headquarters and was determined to seize the Führer when he arrived. Word to this effect was conveyed by Fabian von Schlabrendorff to the British just as they were closing their Embassy on September 3, 1939. But Hitler canceled the promised visit, and, shortly thereafter, again retired Hammerstein.

After Poland was overrun and divided between Germany and Russia, Hitler simultaneously made peace overtures and prepared to invade Holland and Belgium and attack France. Almost all of the General Staff was opposed to a campaign of such magnitude beginning so late in the year. The tank generals, including Guderian, Reichenau and Hoeppner, were unanimous in the belief that ground conditions would hamper mechanized warfare, and the air force generals (including Göring) insisted that the November fogs made impossible an efficacious use of air power. The arguments between Hitler and Keitel on one hand, and Brauchitsch and the Wehrmacht generals on the other, were bitter. Brauchitsch told the conspirators, with whom he was still in touch,

53

that he did not know whether he would arrest Hitler or Hitler would arrest him.

General Beck pressed Halder to take action. Halder vacil lated and excused himself by saying he did not know what Brauchitsch would do. "If Brauchitsch hasn't enough force of character to make a decision," Beck told Halder, "you must make it for him and present him with a *fait accompli*." Halder then replied that internal upheaval would invite attack from the enemy.

Nevertheless, Halder did consult several army group commanders in the field as to whether they would join in urging Brauchitsch to give the orders for Hitler's arrest. The answers from most of the field commanders were unsatisfactory. Witzleben, however, was an exception. He had been transferred from his command of the Berlin military district and put in charge of an army in the West. A member of the conspiracy from the early days, he was prepared to act. Meanwhile Hassell, through his connections in the Vatican, tried —without much success—to find out whether the Allies would refrain from attacking Germany in the event that the removal of Hitler and the Nazi party led to internal disorders. Some such assurance was necessary to meet the objection of the military leaders that a successful plot meant revolution and that revolution would open the door to enemy occupation.

Although the position of many of the military leaders was ambiguous the conspirators were convinced that their opportunity would be gone once Hitler had launched his attack on the West. It was necessary to forestall him. With Witzleben's help Oster, Gisevius and others prepared the plans for another coup against Hitler.

Albrecht von Kessel, who was in the Foreign Office and on the fringes of the conspiracy, in the diary he kept while stationed at the Vatican, gives an interesting version of the failure of this particular plot:

About November 4, 1939, I was told that all was ready for a coup d'état within a few days when Hitler was to make an inspection tour outside Berlin. Even skeptics who had never believed any of the former plans would be executed were convinced this one was really serious. Then on the morning of November 6 I learned the whole thing was off. No reasons were given. I heard the explanation later. On November 5 the general in whose hands all the strings of the plot were held—I did not learn his name and did not ask for it—had to report to Hitler on a routine army matter. At the end of his report Hitler suddenly asked what else he planned. The general, not yet suspicious, mentioned a few further technical details. Thereupon Hitler exclaimed: "No, I don't mean that, I can see by looking at you that you still plan something else." The general, controlling himself with difficulty, pretended surprise and lack of understanding and was graciously dismissed. He hurried in panic to the General Staff and announced that the plot had been betrayed. The plans were abandoned and all possible traces of the conspiracy covered up. Troops that had been held outside Berlin were ordered to move to the western front. After a few days it became evident that there had been no betrayal, that Hitler could not have known of the plot. He had simply tried an "intuitive" shot in the dark.

On November 8 a bomb exploded in the Bürgerbräu in Munich shortly after Hitler left the building following his annual speech commemorating the Beer Hall Putsch of 1923. This still remains a mystery. Some evidence indicates the bomb was planted with the knowledge of Hitler and Himmler in order to solidify a tribal loyalty in the German people, or, like the Reichstag fire, to justify new repressions. I have heard of the existence of photographs showing a high Gestapo officer standing by Hitler with a watch in his hand in order to make sure he got away in time. Others ascribe the attempt to a Communist working independently of any of the anti-Nazi conspirators and without their knowledge. A very recent report declares the plot to have been the work of a Socialist underground group. In any event, the conspirators had to lie low until the storm abated, as of course this attempt at assassination was turned to effective use by the Gestapo.

The date of the invasion of the West was not yet finally fixed but Hitler was preparing to move at any time. (The Nürnberg record discloses that between November 7, 1939, and May 10, 1940, the decision to attack was deferred no less than twelve times. The thirteenth, and fatal, order was given May 9.) On November 23 he called his top military leaders together and gave them an indoctrination speech (penciled notes—short, clipped sentences—of what he said are among the Nürnberg documents): "A people unable to produce the strength to fight must withdraw. Wars today are different from those of 100 years ago. Today we can speak of a racial fight. Today we fight for oil fields, rubber, treasures of the earth, etc. . . . The decision to strike was always in me. Earlier or later I wanted to solve the problem. Under pressure it was decided that the East was to be attacked first."

Then, after referring to the quick victory in Poland, Hitler said the East could be held by a few divisions, that Russia was not dangerous, and that "we have a pact with Russia. Pacts, however, are only kept as long as they serve a purpose." Then he described the necessity to attack England: "The English are a tough enemy, above all on defense." But to attack England effectively and to starve England out it was necessary to get closer to the English coast. Flights to England required so much fuel that effective bomb loads could not be carried. England's commerce was to be destroyed by systematic mining of her sea lanes, as England could not live without its imports. He went on:

The permanent sowing of mines on the English coast will bring England to her knees. However, this can only be done if we have occupied Belgium and Holland. It is a difficult decision for me. No one has ever achieved what I have achieved. My life is of no importance in all this. I have led the German people to a great height, even if the world does hate us now. I am gambling everything. I have to choose between victory and destruction. I choose victory. This is a great historical choice, to be compared with the decision of Frederick the Great before the first Silesian war. Prussia owes its rise to the heroism of one man. Even his closest advisers were disposed to capitulate. Everything depended on Frederick the Great. Even the decisions of Bismarck in 1866 and 1870 were no [?] less important. My decision is unchangeable. I shall attack France and England at the earliest and most favorable moment. Breach of Belgian and Dutch neutrality is meaningless. No one will question that when we have won. We will not violate this neutrality as idiotically as in 1914.

In December General Beck told Ambassador von Hassell that he had done everything he could to induce Brauchitsch to act before the real shooting war in the West began. He had even let Brauchitsch know that he, Beck, was willing to undertake a coup d'état himself if Brauchitsch would give him a free hand. Brauchitsch gave no encouragement. Admiral Canaris, always pessimistic about the military, told Hassell he had given up all hope of action by the generals. On April 3, 1940, Goerdeler showed Hassell a letter in which General Halder confessed that he had come to the opinion that since Britain and France had declared war on Germany [sic] it would have to be fought through and a compromise peace was senseless. Goerdeler said Halder was completely unnerved and had started to cry when his responsibility was mentioned. Hassell, in his diary, summed up the attitude of the generals during that period with this remark: "These generals seem to want the Hitler government itself to order them to overthrow it."

Nevertheless, the conspirators in the German army who continued to work against the Nazis saw to it that warnings reached the Dutch, Belgians, and officials of other countries threatened with invasion. Gisevius's and Schlabrendorff's later statements to me about these efforts were confirmed by Colonel G. J. Sas, the Netherlands Military Attaché in Berlin at the time.

Colonel Sas had known General Oster very well and had his full confidence. The two had lunched together on November 6, 1939, and Oster told Sas the invasion would begin on November 12. Sas went to The Hague to deliver this information in person. But apparently the protests of the generals, particularly those in the Tank and Air Corps, as well as Hitler's hopes to get peace without giving up Poland, had resulted in a postponement, at least until after the new year.

Early in January, 1940, a German courier plane, on the way from Berlin to the Rhineland, made what appeared to be a forced landing on Belgian soil, near the town of Malines. This plane carried detailed German plans for the invasion of Holland and Belgium. Some assert that the forced landing was a subterfuge and that the plane had been sent by an anti-Nazi group to warn the Belgians of the coming invasion. The Belgian authorities quite naturally thought it was a "plant" and did not attribute much importance to it. Göring, however, was haled on the carpet for this carelessness, as were General Oster and the entire German intelligence service. Oster told Colonel Sas that Hitler raged like a wild animal at the delay occasioned by the necessity of changing the invasion plans.*

Colonel Sas had also received from Oster warning that an attack was being planned for January. He passed this word on to his government. The fact that neither the November

---

* In a talk with Mussolini on April 23, 1944, Hitler confirmed this incident as one of several "where one hardly knew whether it was stupidity or madness which had played a part." He admitted that saboteurs had damaged the war effort but ascribed the airplane affair to lack of foresight. "A man who had received a certain assignment had, with all the papers on the subject, set out on a journey in a Storch plane and landed in Belgium. The documents which the man had taken with him consisted of the plans for our march through Belgium. Such and similar cases had happened in Russia in the neighborhood of Voronezh and Velikie Luki." Hitler added "often human fallibility really celebrated a holiday."

nor the January attacks came off as predicted undoubtedly lessened the effect of Sas's timely warning a few months later.

When, early in 1940, Hitler informed the General Staff that he planned to invade Norway, the generals were opposed on the ground that preparations for the invasion could not possibly be concealed and the British fleet would never let the Germans reach Norway. Halder and Brauchitsch refused to work on the plans. Hitler then turned to his own general staff, composed wholly of men he dominated—Keitel, Jodl, and General Warlimont. This new Nazi staff was eager to invade Norway because, among other reasons, they wanted to try out Germany's new paratroop and airborne divisions. They assured the Führer Norway would be easy.

Again General Oster warned Colonel Sas. The two were meeting frequently, which was not as difficult as one might imagine. For such purposes the black-out is a blessing, as I myself learned in Switzerland. The Dutch Military Attaché used to visit General Oster after dark at his home in a rather secluded Berlin suburb. Ten days before April 9, 1940, the date of the attack upon Norway and Denmark, Oster gave Sas some of the details of the invasion plans. Colonel Sas told me that he informed the Danish Naval Attaché that same night. But the Danes simply did not believe it. They could have done little to prevent or retard the invasion anyway. However, according to Colonel Sas, the Germans learned that the Danes had been warned of the invasion and had instigated a thorough investigation, but fortunately neither Sas nor Oster was found out. For some unknown reason the Belgian Embassy was suspected.

After the attack on Norway but before the invasion of the Lowlands and France, the military conspirators, on the initiative of General Beck, communicated with the former German Chancellor, Joseph Wirth, a convinced anti-Nazi who was living in exile in Switzerland, and asked Wirth to make use of certain Anglo-French contacts he had to ascertain the intentions of the Western powers in the event that a military putsch succeeded in overthrowing Hitler. An ambiguous, noncommital answer arrived just as the offensive in the West began.

Meanwhile, the conspirators made some fruitless attempts to convince individual field commanders of inevitable defeat if Hitler attacked the Low Countries and France. General Thomas made a round of the generals, Leeb, Bock, Rundstedt, Manstein, and Sodenstern, and urged them to refuse to attack Holland and Belgium. In the ensuing crisis, Thomas assured them, the Berlin garrison would arrest Hitler and the army would take over. The generals listened politely. They had won great victories in Poland and Norway and, intoxicated by the prospect of conquering all Europe, they knew better than to believe the eternal skeptics and critics of Adolf Hitler. They also knew the Maginot Line's extension along the Belgian frontier was a farce. Let the panzers roll!

Colonel Sas told me that Oster informed him on May 3 that the attack would begin on May 10. On May 4 Sas received an inquiry from his government asking him to confirm a warning received from The Hague's representative at the Vatican.

On the Sunday before the attack the wife of a German police official called up Sas and told him her husband would travel to Holland in a few days. Sas reported to his government that so far as he could learn the attack was set for Friday. Dutch suspicions were confirmed by the fact that the same officials who had played a sinister role in the invasion of Poland had applied for visas for the Netherlands.

On Thursday, May 9, the atmosphere in the government district of Berlin was tense. Sas and Oster met for the last time in their lives. Oster confirmed once more that the order for the attack in the West had been given. They dined together. "It was like a funeral meal," Sas told me.

After dinner Oster went to the War Ministry in the Bendlerstrasse to see whether any changes had occurred. There had been none. "The swine [Oster's customary way of referring to his Führer] has gone to the western front," Oster told Sas. "I hope we see each other after the war." But this was not to be. General Oster was implacable in his desire to destroy Hitler, Colonel Sas told me, and probably expected to perish in the attempt. Like his chief, Canaris, he was a fatalist, and like him was executed by the Nazis. Colonel Sas recalled having heard Oster say to his family: "Children, children, what a sunny youth you have had. What more do you expect from life?"

When he left Oster, Colonel Sas warned his own minister and the Belgian Military Attaché. Much to his surprise, after twenty minutes they were able to get The Hague on the telephone and to say, in code: "Tomorrow, at dawn, hold tight."

After Holland, Belgium, Luxembourg, and France had been overrun and Hitler returned to Berlin in triumph, the generals who had warned that his aggressions would be a catastrophe for Germany appeared to have been imbeciles. It would require an actual catastrophe to break the spell Hitler had cast over the German people and the German army.

The world awaited a German invasion of the British Isles. Intoxicated by his conquest of France and confident that England would capitulate, Hitler hesitated. The speed of his conquests had upset his time table. The fleet for the invasion of England was not ready as fall turned to winter. Meanwhile the air battle of Britain had been won by the unforgettable R.A.F. Without control of the air the invasion of Britain was impossible. An unconquered Britain meant a long war, and a long war would require more Ukrainian wheat and Caucasian oil than Russia would give—no matter what further concessions Hitler would make.

Late in 1940, probably even before his stormy Berlin meeting with Molotov over Balkan policy, Hitler ordered secret preparations for the destruction of Russia. The General Staff was not 'then informed. (According to the Nürnberg evidence of Field Marshal von Paulus the original directives for the invasion of Russia were issued on December 12, 1940.)

Early in 1941 General Henning von Tresckow, one of the boldest of the conspirators, was appointed to the staff of the Central Army Group, which was soon to be used on the Russian front. Schlabrendorff joined him as his adjutant. Tresckow saw an opportunity to revive a military putsch.

A number of prominent staff officers were extremely skeptical about the Russian adventure. Brauchitsch and even Göring had warned against it. The accurate reports of the German Military Attaché in Moscow, General von Koestring, and the picture of conditions in the Soviet Union presented by the Abwehr, under Admiral Canaris, made many generals respect Russian military and economic strength. Moreover, there had always been a certain amount of pro-Russian sentiment in the German Reichswehr. But Hitler had so often made fools of the generals and their warnings, that they did not defend their doubts with real conviction.

The Russian campaign was set for the beginning of May. The "obstinate attitude" of the Yugoslavs and Greeks delayed the invasion for six weeks.

Some days before the invasion of Russia the conspirators learned that orders had been issued to the German High Command to wage warfare in Russia in total disregard of the rules of war. Hassell noted in his diary that on June 16 (1941) he, Beck, Oster, Goerdeler and Popitz had discussed how they could use these orders to convince Germany's military leaders of the dangers of Hitler's inhuman policy. They concluded that Brauchitsch, Halder and others were too weak to do anything to thwart Hitler's determination to involve the army in his policy of murder and arson—which so far had been the province of the SS. "Hopeless corporals," Hassell called them. General Beck protested to Brauchitsch and told him that General von Bock, commander of the Central Army Group, had actually refused to pass on the murderous order and that a number of army commanders had followed Bock's lead. But Hassell could only note in his diary: "It is despairing, indeed, that such a thing has to be done in an unorganized manner and peters out without being utilized for a coup."

Tresckow and Schlabrendorff were able to build a certain following within the staff at the Central Army Group headquarters, but not, as they hoped, to induce Bock to oppose the invasion of Russia. However, a great turning point in the war came when the Germans were stopped in front of Moscow. Even though Guderian's tanks were frozen, Hitler ordered a mad and costly offensive. The General Staff was in ferment and the conspirators thought their chance to overthrow Hitler had surely come. But all that happened was that Brauchitsch and Guderian were relieved of their commands. Hitler took over. In the course of subsequent changes the command of the Central Army Group was taken from Bock and given to Kluge.

From the day of Kluge's appointment Tresckow and his friends started to work on him. In a way Kluge was afraid of his subordinate. Whenever Tresckow was present, Kluge was the perfect anti-Nazi, willing to act at the first opportunity. When Tresckow was out of sight the Field Marshal faltered.

Tresckow's influence over Kluge did not depend only on personality. Tresckow had evidence that the Field Marshal had received from Hitler 250,000 marks—out of the Führer's personal funds, tax-free, unrecorded—and the almost equally precious gift of permission to build a house on his estate when even some of the top Nazis could not obtain building material and labor. Tresckow kept dinning in Kluge's ear that he could atone for the eternal shame of accepting a bribe from Hitler only by becoming the man who rescued Germany from the Nazi tyranny.

Sometime in 1942 the anti-Nazi officers on the eastern front coordinated their efforts with the conspirators in Berlin. Through General Oster, whom he had known for some time, Schlabrendorff—and later Tresckow—met General Friedrich Olbricht, Chief of Staff of the Replacement Army, who was helping Oster build an organization in Berlin, Vienna, Cologne and Munich for the day when Hitler was overthrown. Tresckow was sure the German armies would soon meet with disaster in the East and that defeat could be exploited to turn the armies in the field against Hitler. Goerdeler, Hassell, and other civilians were drawn into these discussions with the officers of the eastern front, who put themselves at the disposal of Goerdeler's group. On one occasion Goerdeler, provided with false papers by his Abwehr friends, visited Field Marshal von Kluge at his headquarters at Smolensk.

By the end of 1942 the conspirators felt that the situation was shaping to their purpose. The British victory at El Aiamein was followed on November 8 by the invasion of North Africa. A few days later the counterattacks began that wrought the German disaster at Stalingrad, and the Russian steam roller began moving in earnest.

The plan was for several army groups in the East, with Kluge taking the lead, to announce that the situation had become so desperate they would take no orders from Hitler. Field Marshal von Witzleben, then commander in the West, was to follow with a similar announcement. Reliable Replacement Army troops, under Beck and Olbricht, were to occupy Berlin and other key cities, and arrest the Gestapo and party leaders.

It was decided that the first announcement should come from the commander of the most threatened unit—from Colonel General von Paulus of the Sixth Army still fighting at Stalingrad. Two of Paulus's generals, Walther von Seydlitz and Alexander Edler von Daniels, tried for weeks to persuade Paulus to refuse to follow Hitler's intuition. The Soviets had started an encircling counteroffensive and the Sixth Army was cut off from most of its supply bases. Paulus knew he needed 120 tons of munitions a day and was getting forty; he needed 100 tons of food—not twenty; and 60 tons of gasoline instead of from ten to twenty. He knew also that an immediate retreat was imperative. But the Führer willed that the Sixth Army should hold.

Finally Paulus consented to fly to Hitler and tell him of the Sixth Army's desperate plight. Hitler promised him a field marshal's baton and he returned in time to be captured by the Russians. Seydlitz continued his arguments with Paulus behind the barbed wire of a Soviet war prisoner camp and Paulus, whose revolt was to have been the signal for an anti-Hitler putsch by Germans in Germany, had to be content with working with the Free Germany Committee in Moscow.

The battle of Stalingrad, one great turning point of the war, revealed to all but the most fanatical Nazis the absurdity of Hitler's military leadership. However, when General Thomas suggested to Keitel that Hitler must be told that the morale of the German people was rapidly declining because of the senseless sacrifices at Stalingrad, Keitel replied: "The Führer is not interested in such considerations. It is his conviction that if the German people do not want to understand him and fight, they will have to perish." On an earlier report which Thomas had given Keitel for Hitler's information, Keitel wrote: "I hereby forbid that such reports be shown to the Führer. They do more harm than good. The standing of the OKW with the Führer is only adversely affected by them and the person of General Thomas is further compromised. The Führer has other sources of information and would rather believe these than his generals."

And the generals? After the surrender at Stalingrad it was decided that Kluge and Manstein * should fly to Hitler's headquarters and demand, as a minimum price for continued service, that the Führer make them Supreme Commanders in the East. If he refused they would openly rebel. But Hitler wrapped them both around his little finger. He made small concessions, was charming and reasonable, and they never even came to the point.

The failure of the "Stalingrad putsch," as it was called, made it clear that even in the face of military catastrophe the generals could not be counted upon. Beck, who had foreseen the Stalingrad disaster in all its details, vowed he would court-martial Paulus and the other generals after Hitler was overthrown. "These cowards make an anti-militarist out of me, an old soldier," he remarked. He agreed that assassination was now the only way and Tresckow, Schlabrendorff and their group offered to do it.

Before this decision was made, Tresckow, through friendship with General Schmundt, Hitler's adjutant, had been able to arrange for Hitler to visit Central Army Group headquarters in Smolensk. The idea at that time was for Kluge to provoke a quarrel with Hitler and arrest him and his entire staff. A cavalry regiment under Colonel von Boeselager was prepared to make the arrests. Kluge was to seize power temporarily and it was hoped that a *fait accompli* would compel the other commanders in the East to support him. Hitler's visit was postponed time and again, and Kluge weak-

* When General von Manstein had been approached and asked if he would join Paulus and the other eastern-front generals in refusing to obey Hitler, he indicated he was not averse to the idea, but wanted to capture Sebastopol first. The military problem intrigued him—and might bring him another decoration.

ened. "The German soldiers and the world would not understand," he explained.

However, this no longer mattered after assassination was decided upon.

Hitler finally came, on March 13, 1943, and at a congenial supper party Tresckow asked one of Hitler's adjutants if he would be kind enough to take two bottles of cognac back to the Führer's headquarters for General Stieff. The adjutant consented and Schlabrendorff saw the package safely into Hitler's plane.

The package contained the same type of bomb Stauffenberg used more than a year later.

As Hitler's plane soared into the sky Tresckow and Schlabrendorff had every reason to believe they, and Germany, had seen the last of the obsessed Austrian. They informed Kluge and waited for word of the "airplane disaster." In Berlin General Olbricht awaited the call of Schlabrendorff to set the putsch machinery going.

Two hours later they learned that Hitler had arrived at his destination.

Their disappointment was overwhelming, but they had no time to waste on despair. If the package with the explosive was discovered every anti-Nazi on the eastern front would hang.

Schlabrendorff took the first courier plane and flew to the Führer's headquarters. He was in time and retrieved the package. When he opened it that night in a private compartment of a train to Berlin, he discovered that the bomb had been properly set, the little capsule containing the acid had been broken, the acid had eaten through the wire, and the firing pin had shot forward. But the percussion cap had not gone off. "Disappointment and joy both welled up in me," he later told me, "disappointment because this really unforeseeable accident frustrated the assassination, joy because we had been able to prevent the disclosure of our action and all the possible consequences."

Schlabrendorff's luck in retrieving the bomb followed him after his arrest a year and a quarter later. He was, of course, badly compromised by the events of July 20, but he was not tried until February, 1945. Then, as his trial before the presiding judge of the People's Court, Judge Freisler, was approaching its end, American bombers, raiding Berlin in daylight, forced the court to adjourn to its underground shelter. A direct hit on the courthouse weakened the supports of the shelter and a beam fell on Freisler's head and mortally wounded him. In the melee the record of Schlabrendorff's trial and much of the evidence against him was lost. When he was again tried the new judge lacked both the evidence and the sadistic zeal of Freisler, and Schlabrendorff got off with confinement in a concentration camp. As the Allies closed in on Germany Schlabrendorff was moved southward from camp to camp and finally fell into the hands of the Fifth American Army when, coming up through Italy, it reached the north-Italian Alps.

The failure of the assassination attempts caused some of the conspirators to doubt whether they were following the proper course. Some, like General Thomas for example, argued that as it was now quite apparent that the war was lost and that no new government could secure anything better than unconditional surrender, a putsch might be interpreted at home and abroad as merely the act of ambitious generals to seize power and would make Hitler a martyr in German eyes. This would be worse than total defeat. Tresckow and his group differed with Thomas. Hitler must be assassinated, they said. It was not the immediate political results which were important but the fact that the German anti-Nazis could prove in this way, and in this way alone, to the world and to posterity, that they were ready to risk their lives to remove Hitler. Compared to this all else was secondary.

68

When later, sometime in 1943, Colonel von Stauffenberg found his way into the inner circle of the conspiracy, vacillation over assassination ceased. Throughout the remainder of 1943, as the military situation worsened, more and more young officers became convinced that Hitler must be killed. The Badoglio coup d'état in Italy, of which the German conspirators were informed in advance, gave the plotters new hope.

On December 26, 1943, Stauffenberg, who had been maneuvered into a position in the Replacement Army that gave him access to Hitler's conferences, carried a bomb in his briefcase to Hitler's headquarters. But the conference was canceled without explanation at the last moment.

In January, 1944, another ingenious attempt was planned by the Tresckow group. A new uniform was to be demonstrated before Hitler. Tresckow found three young German officers who volunteered to be the models and to carry in their field packs explosives which would kill Hitler—and themselves. Among the young officers was the son of Ewald von Kleist, prominent anti-Nazi Conservative—then twenty-one years old—who was to sacrifice himself with the consent of his father. The preparations were extensive. But an air raid intervened and the demonstration was indefinitely postponed. Young Kleist survives; his father was executed.

This was the last attempt of which there is any record until July 20, 1944. With each passing month Hitler became more and more inaccessible, and unbelievable precautions were taken to prevent anyone but the most trusted Nazis and his own staff officers from approaching him.

6. The Abwehr

An intelligence service is the ideal vehicle for a conspiracy. Its members can travel about at home and abroad under secret orders, and no questions are asked. Every scrap of paper in the files, its membership, its expenditure of funds, its contacts, even enemy contacts, are state secrets. Even the Gestapo could not pry into the activities of the Abwehr until Himmler absorbed it. He only succeeded in doing so late in 1943.

The Military Intelligence Division of the OKW (the unified German High Command), charged with espionage and counterintelligence for the German armed forces, was called Spionage Abwehr, or Abwehr for short. *Abwehr* in German means "to ward off," but far from being merely a defensive organization, the Abwehr had, of course, many offensive uses. For years it had been quite separate from the various intelligence and spy organizations of the Nazi party, such as the Gestapo and the infamous Security Service (Sicherheitsdienst—SD), which were ultimately combined in the Central Security Office (Reichssicherheitshauptamt), which had a foreign intelligence service of its own. Until the Abwehr was taken under Himmler's "protective" wing there was constant jealousy between the Abwehr and the party intelligence organization, the SD.

The Abwehr had charge, among other things, of the fifth column activities that supported German military operations, and of commandos, sabotage and espionage behind enemy lines. As is well known, the Germans did not hesitate to dress their agents in enemy uniforms in order to create confusion in enemy territory. The Abwehr also directed the notorious Brandenburg Division, which was largely composed of spies, commandos and saboteurs, and was constantly used, particularly on the eastern front.

But certain key members of the Abwehr deliberately falsified secret reports to deceive Hitler; crossed some of Hitler's most important and diabolical plans; saved some big and little enemies of Hitler from the Gestapo; and aided and protected the conspirators who were determined to kill Hitler and overthrow the Nazis. Why?

There are two answers. First, the Abwehr was in part recruited from young officers, lawyers, business men and landowners, many of whom temperamentally and ideologically were anti-Nazi. The complex personality of the guiding genius and head of the Abwehr, Admiral Wilhelm Canaris, is the second answer.

The enigma of that strange man continues to this day, as Allied intelligence officers still search for the Canaris diaries. They are supposed to contain important secrets in the history of the Third Reich. Germans continue to spread the rumor that Canaris is not really dead. Such rumors seem to me refuted by the testimony of a Danish intelligence officer, Hans Lunding, who occupied a cell next to that of the Admiral in the Flossenbürg concentration camp. He stated that during the night of April 7, 1945, Canaris had been undressed and hanged in the prison court. The same information was confirmed by Schlabrendorff, who was a prisoner there during that April, and who was told by a guard that Canaris had been hanged by special order of Himmler. Canaris' deputy chief in the Abwehr, General Oster, was executed at the same time. In those last days the Nazis were destroying all human, as well as all documentary, evidence of their crimes.

Admiral Canaris came from a family of officials and tradesmen in the Mosel and Saar districts, and his father had been manager of a small mine. He was of Greek ancestry but the family had lived in Germany for centuries and had become very German—almost chauvinistically so.

During World War I Canaris was a lieutenant commander in the German navy and was interned in South America. He managed to escape to Spain, disguised as a stoker. In Madrid the German military attaché employed him as an agent and Canaris had his first taste of undercover work.

After the war Canaris became a member of the illegal "black Reichswehr" and actively participated in Germany's secret rearmament. He supervised, and camouflaged, the building of German submarines in Holland, Finland, and Spain. For these activities he was bitterly attacked by the parties of the Left. His nationalism made him hostile to the Weimar Republic. The Nazis thought well of him. He became head of the Abwehr in 1935.

Admiral Canaris has always been regarded, outside Germany, as a very dangerous man. Yet he tolerated, protected and at times abetted anti-Nazi conspirators in the Abwehr. His secret service functioned well, and he provided Hitler with valuable information. He also provided Hitler with information colored as Canaris wished it to be. For example, he consistently emphasized the difficulties of a German invasion of Spain and was instrumental in discouraging Hitler from attempting it. And he was the implacable foe of Himmler. Yet Canaris himself did not join the conspiracy.

One of his friends and close collaborators, Major General Erwin Lahousen, an Austrian from the ranks of the Vienna secret service, told the International Tribunal in Nürnberg that Canaris hated "Hitler, his system and particularly his methods. Canaris stated his attitude thus: 'We did not succeed in preventing this war of aggression. The war means the end of Germany and our own end, and as such it is a misfortune and a catastrophe of the greatest proportions. However, a misfortune that would have been even greater than this catastrophe would have been the triumph of Hitler.' "

Lahousen then told of the diary, which he said Canaris kept in order "to inform Germany and the world once and for all of the guilt of those people who were guiding the fate of Germany at this time."

When I was in Berlin in the fall of 1945 I found what seemed to be some good clues as to the location of the Canaris papers. These, I was told, originally included: the diary; a chronology of Nazi crimes from 1933 on, prepared by Hans von Dohnanyi; a card index file of Nazi leaders and their individual crimes; memoranda on the coup d'état prepared by Beck, Goerdeler and Dohnanyi; the record of the trial of General von Fritsch; and memoranda on negotiations between the Vatican and the Beck-Goerdeler plotters.

These papers had all been kept in a safe under Abwehr control at the Zossen military headquarters near Berlin. Later, it appears, some of the papers were buried near a hunting lodge in Hanover which I at first thought I would be able to locate. Unfortunately, the man who had been entrusted with the task of burying the documents, sometime in 1944, had refused to let anyone accompany him. A few months later, after July 20, he was executed and his secret was not passed on to any persons now living. From an interrogation of a German prisoner after the war it was learned that the documents left in Zossen were discovered by the Gestapo and, under the personal supervision of Ernst Kaltenbrunner, who succeeded Heydrich as head of the SD, had been taken to a castle, Schloss Mittersill in the Tyrol, and there burnt one by one. The prisoner declared that the destroyed documents included the full Canaris diary and also the Vatican and Fritsch papers. I am now convinced Canaris's invaluable diary and the other records have been irretrievably lost.

But parts of Lahousen's contributions to Canaris's diary have been found. Brittle and discolored, unearthed from a secret hiding place, they have been carefully restored and were presented to the Nürnberg Tribunal. From these papers Lahousen reconstructed the history of some of Canaris's attempts to frustrate Hitler's designs.

According to Lahousen, Admiral Canaris tried to dissuade Hitler from extermination policies in Poland and later in Russia, and protested against violations of the laws of war regarding prisoners. He refused, in the winter of 1940, to carry out an order to have General Maxime Weygand, then in North Africa, assassinated. When General Henri Giraud escaped from prison in Königstein with the help of the French underground intelligence service, Keitel urged that he be assassinated by Canaris's men. Canaris did nothing, and when Keitel asked him about it, Canaris said Heydrich of the SD had made preparations for the murder. This was not true, but it was a safe excuse since Heydrich had been killed at Lidice in Czechoslovakia the day after Giraud fled.

Lahousen made one very significant remark in his Nürnberg testimony. The Abwehr chiefs, including a Colonel Pieckenbrock, one of Canaris's closest associates, were discussing what they should do about the order to kill Giraud. Pieckenbrock spoke up and said, according to Lahousen, that "it was about time Keitel was told to inform Hitler, his Hitler, that the military Abwehr is no murder organization like the SD and the SS." Canaris did tell Keitel and, according to Lahousen, reported back to his associates that it was understood that the Abwehr was to be left out of the murder business.

The "Little Greek"—a nickname given Canaris because of his Levantine appearance—was a short, thin man, a bundle of vibrant nerves. He was an insatiable reader and loathed paper work and all bureaucracy. His overwhelming interest was human nature and how to control it—no matter by what means. He was a pessimist, a fatalist and a mystic. He came to believe he should not try to interfere too forcibly with the course of history. He foresaw the terrible end of the German nation but was unwilling himself to take direct action to prevent it because, as Hans Gisevius said, "he thought with an agonized feeling of guilt that it would be the just punishment for the crimes of the Nazis." Perhaps Canaris also felt a personal sense of guilt for opposing the Weimar Republic and thus helping Hitler to power. He had put his faith in reactionaries and militarists, and now knew them by their fruits.

Kessel's diary contains this portrait of Canaris:

Flexible, cunning and sensitive. Full of interest in foreign political developments and usually extremely well informed; the ideal chief of a "deuxième bureau." Aside from this a kind man who took every opportunity to pry a victim from the Gestapo. For us younger men he always showed particular consideration. His hatred of the Nazis was coupled with an inborn love of intrigue; wherever there seemed to be a plot in the making he was informed about it and—involved. On the other hand, in the opinion of some of my friends, he also had the faults of his profession, a lack of seriousness which does not want to tie itself down definitely but juggles with all possibilities.

General Halder thought him "the sort of man from whom you learned things and who was in touch with people you did not want to meet in public. I would describe Canaris as the man who instigated but never gave the final shape to things." And an angered Gestapo official told one of the few survivors of the putsch: "He pulled the wool over the eyes of all of them, Heydrich, Himmler, Keitel, Ribbentrop, and even the Führer."

I do not mean to give the impression that the entire Ger-

75

man Abwehr spent its time plotting against Hitler. Nothing would be farther from the truth. Probably ninety-five per cent or more of the Abwehr was collecting intelligence about, and plotting against, the Allies. Possibly some five per cent of its personnel, including several of the top men, were anti-Nazis and had a loose organization of their own through which they helped the conspiracy. General Oster, chief of the Abwehr's personnel, belonged to the inner circle of the conspirators. He could not keep fanatical Nazis out of the Abwehr, but he got as many anti-Nazis into it as he could. Few of these were professional military men, although some were drafted and plotted in uniform.

After the Fritsch affair in 1938 Oster also became the trusted adviser of the non-Nazi generals. He informed them in advance of Hitler's and Himmler's plans, as the Nazis often intentionally kept the old-line generals in the dark, even about actions in which the generals were to participate.

Oster's chief assistant, Hans von Dohnanyi, a former judge and a civilian, was closely associated in the conspiracy with a group of young German intellectuals, churchmen and business men, including his four brothers-in-law: Justus Delbrück, a government official in the days of the Republic and a business man in the Third Reich; the brothers Claus and Dietrich Bonhoeffer—Claus was an attorney for the German air lines and Dietrich a Protestant clergyman who had been in charge of the German church in London; and Rüdiger Schleicher, legal expert in the Air Ministry. All of these men worked under the cover of the Abwehr. All of them were executed "for participation in the plot of 20 July," except Justus Delbrück, who was arrested by the Russians shortly after they liberated him from the Lehrterstrasse prison in Berlin. He has not been heard of since.

Before the outbreak of the war, the Abwehr supplied much of the material used in the attempts to convince generals, and even some Nazis, that an attack upon Poland would certainly lead to war with England, and France as well. The Abwehr also gave some consideration to a prewar plan to arrest Hitler on the technicality that he was insane and to appoint Göring successor and "preserver of the peace." This was the type of intrigue that would appeal to Canaris. It was a subtle way at least to delay the war. Göring's secret prewar peace efforts were based on the premise that Germany should not go to war until *1941*. Canaris tried to strengthen Göring's position and alienate him from the other top Nazis. Göring's monumental vanity made him very susceptible. The heights his vanity attained were related with relish at the Nürnberg trials by his former cabinet colleague, Hjalmar Schacht:

Hitler I call an amoral type, but Göring I can only regard as immoral and criminal. By nature endowed with a certain bon-hommie which he managed to exploit for his own popularity, he was the most egocentric being imaginable. The assumption of political power was for him only a means for personal enrichment and personal good living. The success of others filled him with envy. His greed knew no bounds. His predilection for jewels, gold and finery was unimaginable. He knew no comrade-ship. Only so long as someone was useful to him was he friends with him, but only on the surface. Göring's knowledge in all fields equaled zero, especially in the economic field. Of all the economic matters which Hitler entrusted to him in the autumn of 1936 he had not the faintest notion, though he created an im-mense official apparatus and misused his powers as lord of all economy most outrageously. In his personal appearance he was so theatrical that you could only compare him with Nero. A lady who had tea with his second wife reported that he appeared at this tea in a sort of Roman toga and sandals studded with jewels, his hands bedecked with jeweled rings and other orna-ments, his face painted and his lips rouged.

Göring was certainly a thoroughgoing brigand, and would not have hesitated to eliminate Hitler if he had felt he could succeed him, but even the intrigues of a Canaris could not have accomplished this. Schacht's comments, while quite accurate as to Göring's vanity and criminality, and his ignorance in the field of economics are tinged with jealousy. Göring was no fool where strategy and his chosen field of aviation were concerned, as any of the Army interrogators who questioned him would willingly admit. If Hitler, in 1940-41, had listened to Göring's counsel to invade Spain and North Africa rather than Russia the war might have lasted far longer than it did. Certainly the plotters in the Abwehr never felt safe in discounting Göring, and for their own purposes tried, but with little success, to sharpen the rivalry for power which separated him from Himmler. The latter's competing intelligence service was an ever present threat to the existence of the Abwehr, and seriously inconvenienced General Oster's program for using the Abwehr's agents in neutral countries to establish contacts for the conspirators outside Germany.

Even before the war contact had been made with the British in Berlin. Goerdeler's travels have already been mentioned, and just before the outbreak of war Schlabrendorff went to London and informed Winston Churchill and Lord Lloyd of what he had learned about the Hitler-Stalin pact, of the plans of the anti-Nazi conspiracy within Germany, and of the certainty of an attack upon Poland. After war broke out, Oster created contacts for the conspiracy in Sweden, Switzerland, Spain and Turkey. For example, when in 1942 the Lutheran pastor, Dietrich Bonhoeffer, traveled to Sweden to give the Bishop of Chichester a message for the British Government, he did so with papers prepared by the Abwehr. One of Oster's best contacts abroad—on behalf of the conspiracy—was the Catholic lawyer Josef Müller, who was the secular agent of Cardinal Faulhaber at the Vatican. He was caught by the Nazis in 1943, but survived a long imprisonment and at the time of this writing is active politically in Munich as head of the Bavarian Christian Social Union Party.

"Illegal" activities in the Abwehr increased as time went on, but they were threatened by Himmler's desire to get all intelligence, domestic and foreign, under his control. He constantly looked for any excuse to intrigue against Canaris and the Abwehr as a whole. He found one late in 1943. The Gestapo discovered that Dohnanyi was involved in unauthorized foreign-currency transactions (the real purpose of which was to provide for people who had to take refuge abroad). Himmler used this information as a basis to blackmail Canaris and destroy the Abwehr. In these efforts he found a surprising ally in Göring, who recently had had in his own Air Ministry the *Rote Kapelle* scandal, described later. Naturally Göring was anxious to divert public attention to other scandals. A Nazi official of extreme cunning and ability named Roeder, had been in charge of the *Rote Kapelle* investigation. Göring had Roeder appointed to investigate the Abwehr. He was also intent on proving that the army and the church were plotting together against the party.

The situation of the conspirators became extremely serious. Oster, involved at the very outset when he refused to agree to Dohnanyi's arrest, was afraid the Gestapo would break into his safe and seize the "illegal" records. He succeeded in saving most of the papers before he was removed from office and put under house arrest. The conspirators' organization within the Abwehr, the result of years of difficult work, was in the greatest jeopardy.

And then, right on top of the Dohnanyi affair, two Abwehr agents in Turkey, Erich Maria Vermehren and his wife, deserted to the Allies. Himmler closed in at once.

Admiral Canaris knew very well what was at stake. With the help of the Judge Advocate of the Germany Army, Dr. Carl Sack, whose participation in the conspiracy later cost him his life, Canaris persuaded Field Marshal Keitel that

Himmler was seeking to control not only the Abwehr but the army. The struggle between Canaris and Himmler ended in a compromise. The investigation was taken out of the hands of Roeder. Oster was forbidden to travel and kept under strict surveillance. Gisevius, threatened with a treason charge, barely succeeded in getting back to his post in Zurich. Canaris himself survived, but was so badly compromised that, on Himmler's insistence, he was forced into retirement.

Before he retired he appointed as Oster's successor Colonel Georg Hansen, who completely shared Oster's views. Hansen was not then suspected, and even after the Abwehr was absorbed into Himmler's revamped and Nazified secret service and put under the immediate control of Kaltenbrunner, Hansen was able to maintain some contact with the conspirators, both in Germany and abroad. He continued to do so until July 20, when he too was discovered and hanged.

The break-up of the Abwehr late in 1943 was the most serious blow the conspirators had experienced up to that time. In General Oster they lost one of their coolest heads and most careful planners. In addition, they lost their most effective cover and their surest means of communication with each other and the outside world. If the Abwehr could have kept its independent existence for six months more, the disintegration of morale in the officer corps could have been turned to good account. Ways and means might have been found, through the means of communication available to the Abwehr, to effect a Wehrmacht surrender to the Allies. In the summer of 1944 several of the front-line generals were ready to call it quits, but there was no way to establish contact between them and the Allies. The Abwehr alone had the tools required to do this. Those who are disposed to stress the "efficiency" of dictatorships would do well to ponder the interesting fact that in Hitler's totalitarian state the four top men of the German intelligence service—Admiral Canaris, General Oster, Dohnanyi, and Colonel Hansen—and scores of their subordinates had to be executed for treason.

7. The Kreisau Circle

The Abwehr furnished the technical facilities for the conspiracy, its lines of communication, contacts with foreign countries, and the cover under which the individual conspirators could operate. It was the Kreisau Circle, led by Count Helmuth von Moltke, which provided the spiritual and political ideology. Even today the proposals evolved by these men must be considered seriously by anyone concerned with the future of Germany.

The Circle took its name from the Moltke estate at Kreisau in Upper Silesia, where the group frequently met in secret to plan for the Germany which would follow the collapse of Hitler. It included men—for the most part relatively young men—from widely different walks of life. Some bore names famous in Prussian and German history, but the general tone of the Circle was far from reactionary. There were Protestants and Catholics, professional men, churchmen, militant Socialists and men of the Right. There was some disagreement among them as to where they should look for support, to the East or the West. Moltke's contacts were almost exclusively with the West, but some of his friends and active members of the Circle were greatly influenced by Russia. But all were united in opposing Nazism, even though they realized, as Moltke wrote to an English friend in 1942, that the success of their efforts would mean the total collapse of Germany as a national unit. "We are ready to face this," he said, but "we can only expect to get our people to overthrow this reign of terror and horror if we are able to show a picture beyond the terrifying and hopeless immediate future."

The Nazis came to have a wholesome fear of the men of the Kreisau Circle because its opposition was based on moral and religious grounds. In the course of the trials of the conspirators in the People's Court Presiding Judge Roland Freisler declared: "The Moltke Circle made the political preparations for the 20th of July." The motivating force in the plot, he added, was in the men of Kreisau rather, even, than in Goerdeler.

Freisler was one of the most sinister, and little known, of the Nazi personalities. Cruel and cynical, quick-witted and eloquent, Freisler epitomized the brutality of that strange thing the Nazis called "justice." Why they bothered to conduct some of those secret trials is a mystery of Nazi mentality. They were not great spectacles to influence world opinion like the Moscow trials, but were held behind closed doors. The Nazis seemed to enjoy occasionally observing the forms of justice while destroying its substance. During one trial Freisler wanted to refer to the Penal Code but not a single copy could be found in the court!

After some years as State Secretary in the Ministry of Justice Freisler expected to become head of that Ministry. But instead he was given the presidency of the notorious People's Court. Nothing daunted, he set out to make a reputation. He subordinated all human feeling to the dogma of the party, and became the chief proponent of the dictum that individuals should be punished not only for treasonable acts but also for seditious thoughts. He was at his best when he tried members of the Kreisau group. *Bluturteile über Bluturteile*—blood judgment after blood judgment—was handed down by Freisler, the Robespierre of the Nazi revolution, as he was sometimes called. His court was such a mockery of justice that reputable lawyers did everything possible to avoid the necessity of defending cases before him.

Until his death—the result of an American raid on Berlin —Freisler presided over many of the trials of those involved in July 20. The stenographic transcript of the first of these trials, that of Field Marshal Erwin von Witzleben, General Helmuth Stieff, General Erich Hoeppner, Count Peter Yorck von Wartenburg and others, came into my hands after hostilities ceased and I was in Berlin running down every clue to the underground I could find. I was fortunate in having the help of my friend Wolf Von Eckardt, then in the American Army and attached to the intelligence staff of the occupation forces in Berlin. Eckardt located a certain Peter Vossen, one of the court stenographers at the July 20 trials, who had recognized the importance of his shorthand notes and preserved them in a safe place. It was about all that he had saved out of the wreckage of Berlin. Later we found a movie of the entire trial. Every detail of the brutal proceedings had been photographed. The original film was some thirty miles long. Goebbels' Propaganda Ministry cut this down to about nine miles. Parts of the film, especially those depicting the hanging of the military conspirators, had been shown by the Nazis to some German army units apparently as an object lesson. The reaction was the opposite of that expected, and there were demonstrations against the showings. When the film was run at a cadet school in Potsdam, everyone, as if by command, turned his back to the screen. The film was quickly withdrawn from even this limited circulation. But it was saved, for Goebbels intended to show it after the war under the title: "They would have deprived us of victory."

The first trials took only two days (August 7 and 8, 1944), and attendance was limited to a handful of picked Nazis. The movie proved that nothing had been left undone to present the prisoners in the worst possible light. They were unshaven, in ill-fitting, ragged civilian clothes, and their physical condition revealed something of what had happened to them in prison. Field Marshal von Witzleben, for example, had been given a pair of trousers many sizes too large, and no suspenders. Whenever he became engrossed in defending himself and gestured, his trousers fell, and his humiliation as he pulled them up was meticulously photographed.

Of the eight who appeared before Freisler on those hot August days the bravest and most forthright was also the youngest—Peter Yorck von Wartenburg, a leading member of the Kreisau Circle. Even Freisler was impressed and remarked: "There is but one man in this group who did not lie—Peter Yorck von Wartenburg." Yorck made no effort to evade responsibility and did not ask for mercy. He fought the Nazis to the end. Here is a significant passage from his testimony:

YORCK: Mr. President, I have already stated during my interrogation that the National Socialist ideology was such that I . . .

FREISLER (interrupting): could not agree. Put concisely, you declared on the question of the Jews that you disagreed with their extermination? You disagreed with the National Socialist conception of justice.

YORCK: The decisive factor which brings together all these questions is the totalitarian claim of the state on the individual which forces him to renounce his moral and religious obligations to God.

This statement contains the essence of the ideas motivating the members of the Kreisau Circle, which originally was a group of close friends, and became, under the Nazis, a political movement containing men ready to risk their lives for their beliefs. Today there are only a few male survivors of the Kreisau Circle, which included some of the best of Germany's young generation.

Peter Yorck was a direct descendant of the famous Count

Yorck von Wartenburg, the Prussian general who ostensibly disobeyed his King and made the secret Tauroggen pact with the Russians in 1812. By uniting with the Russians Count Yorck had abetted the war of liberation against Napoleon. He was considered a traitor in Prussia until his policy proved successful. The "treason" of his descendant a hundred years later stirred the minds of many who knew this background of family history.

Like most of the Kreisau Circle, Yorck was not a professional soldier. He was born in 1904, studied law and political science in Bonn and Breslau, and worked in the civil service in Berlin until he was drafted shortly before the war began. He was in the Polish campaign, and was then transferred to the eastern division of the economic warfare branch of the German War Office. This proved to be a point of vantage from which he could work against the Nazis. When Helmuth von Moltke was arrested in January, 1944, Peter Yorck took over the leadership of the Kreisau Circle.

Moltke, six feet seven inches tall, and striking in physical appearance, was a natural leader of men. He dominated, without arbitrarily forcing his opinions, the circle gathered around him. He was born in 1906, a great grandnephew of the Field Marshal of 1870, and his mother, Dorothy Rose-Innes, was the daughter of a Chief Justice of the Transvaal.

After studying law, Moltke found that his real interest lay in social and political problems rather than at the bar. His fortune disappeared in the inflation, and the ancestral estate given the Field Marshal as a reward for his military victories passed for a time under the control of his creditors. Moltke eventually got it back and then voluntarily partitioned it among his tenants. His junker neighbors and their organization, the Landbund, bitterly criticized him but he continued on his liberal and progressive course.

In an effort to relieve unemployment, to get German

youth off the streets, and to bring the romantic and often overintellectualized university students into closer contact with workers and farmers, Moltke helped organize the German labor camps. In its original form under the Weimar Republic the German Arbeitsdienst was a voluntary organization much like our own CCC. The Nazis, after they came to power, quickly transformed it into one more agency of indoctrination and preparation for war.

Moltke was uncompromisingly anti-Nazi and anti-fascist by conviction. Typical of this was his action on the day before a state visit by Mussolini to Berlin. Workmen came to Moltke's office on Unter den Linden, along which the procession was to pass, to put up the decorations the whole street was to display. Moltke refused to let the workman use his office and persuaded his fellow tenants to do the same. His building was the only undecorated one on Unter den Linden.

To get free of the stifling atmosphere of the Third Reich, he arranged to be called to the English bar, which gave him a good excuse for many trips to London where his close friends were such men as Lord Lothian, who preceded Halifax in the British Embassy in Washington, and Lionel Curtis, the noted British writer and publicist. Dorothy Thompson was one of the Americans who knew him particularly well. She often cited him as proof that there was "another Germany," and her radio broadcasts to Germany during the war, later published in a book entitled *Listen, Hans,* were addressed to Helmuth von Moltke. To "Hans" she once said:

But whether we would make a difference between Hitlerism and the Germans as a nation would, I told you, depend on what you, Hans, and your friends would do, not only on what you would say. I said that one day you would have to demonstrate by deeds, drastic deeds, where you stood, if the salvation of Germany depended on the answer to that question. And I remember that

I asked you whether you and your friends would ever have the courage to act.

Moltke and his friends were murdered for their courage. The Nazis thought even the rope too good for them. Some of them were strangled to death with piano wire.

During the war Moltke became an expert on international law attached to the General Staff, and worked closely with the Abwehr. He thus had an opportunity to travel out of Germany, particularly to Turkey, where he several times advised the Allies of the attitudes and hopes of anti-Nazi Germans. In the course of his legal work for the General Staff he unremittingly protested against any treatment of prisoners and of civilians in occupied countries, particularly in Russia, that violated the rules of war and The Hague and Geneva Conventions. When, after the invasion of North Africa, Moltke learned that Hitler proposed to shoot as traitors all French who fought on the Allied side, he prepared so strong a legal case against such action that the General Staff abandoned the idea.

Moltke's arrest by the Gestapo on January 19, 1944, was not directly the result of his own anti-Nazi activities. He had learned that the arrest of his friend, Dr. Otto Kiep, was imminent. Kiep and his attractive wife had enjoyed real popularity during their years in the German Embassy in Washington and the Consulate General in New York. They had come to the United States prior to Hitler's advent, but had stayed on until Kiep's anti-Nazi views, and actions, including attendance at a luncheon given in honor of Albert Einstein, resulted in his recall. Soon after their return to Berlin Kiep and his wife became members of a small group of violent anti-Nazis gathered around Frau Hanna Solf, widow of the former Ambassador to Japan. The group also included another of those eventually executed by the Gestapo, Albrecht von Bernstorff, Rhodes scholar, diplomat and banker, and nephew of the Ambassador at Washington in World War I.

Secret information that the Gestapo proposed to clean out this "nest of sedition" * reached Moltke and he tried to warn Kiep. He was too late. Kiep was arrested, tortured and later executed. The Gestapo discovered Moltke's connections with Kiep, and more or less as a preventive measure threw him into jail. There Moltke remained until the disclosures following July 20 implicated the entire Kreisau Circle. Though he had been in prison for the six months preceding Stauffenberg's attempt and hence knew nothing of these plans, Moltke was tried and executed in January, 1945.

Even more than by Moltke, the Kreisau Circle's foreign contacts were developed by Adam von Trott zu Solz, who was only thirty-five years old when he appeared before Judge Freisler and was executed.

Trott was educated at Göttingen and then went to Oxford on a Rhodes scholarship. From his early youth he set his heart on a diplomatic career, had traveled widely and had many American and English friends. On his mother's side he traced his ancestry back to John Jay. (It is interesting to note the leading roles in the conspiracy played by Germans who had ties of blood or culture with the Anglo-Saxon world.)

---

* Among those arrested and later hanged was Fräulein Elisabeth von Thadden, head of a well known girls' school near Heidelberg. A woman of high courage, and the daughter of one of the lay leaders of the Confessional Church, she could not refrain from expressing her abhorrence of Nazism. A young Dr. Reckzeh, who worked in the famous Berlin Charité hospital, endeared himself to her by agreeing with her criticism of the party. During a visit to Berlin she took him to a tea party at Frau Solf's where Dr. Reckzeh took the lead in suggesting that Hitler be overthrown and a discussion of this engrossing topic ensued. Among many others Otto Kiep and Arthur Zarden, a former under-secretary in the Finance Ministry, were present. Reckzeh was a Gestapo agent and it was not long before Hanna Solf and all her guests were arrested. All were executed or committed suicide, with the exception of Frau Solf. She escaped through the intervention of the Japanese Ambassador who declared her execution would cause Germany to lose "face" in Japan.

In 1936 Trott went to the Far East on research work for the Rhodes Foundation, and became acquainted with Dr. Edward C. Carter, the secretary of the Institute for Pacific Relations, of New York. Later, on the invitation of Dr. Carter, he attended a conference of the Institute in the United States. War had meanwhile broken out, but aided by Dr. Carter and Trott's cousin William J. Schieffelin, he tried to impress upon some influential circles in the United States what the Nazi ideology portended for the world. He also told them that Hitler could be eliminated only by the anti-Nazi generals, and that they would move only if there was encouragement from outside. As in the case of Goerdeler's visit to the United States, what Trott had to say was received for the most part with either apathy or suspicion.

When Trott returned to Germany he was taken into the Foreign Office and from time to time traveled to neutral countries, chiefly Sweden and Switzerland. On these trips he usually had a message for some Allied representatives. It was on his return from a trip to Sweden, where he had been in touch with Madame Alexandra Michajlowna Kollontay, the Soviet Ambassadress, that he was arrested by the Gestapo.

It was not unnatural that Trott should have been sent to establish relations with Russia. From his early youth he had been deeply interested both in the East and in Marxism. Kessel's diary contains this glimpse of Trott's early radicalism:

I had met him ten years earlier [1929] in Berlin, where he attracted attention with his doctor's thesis on Hegel. He was then still very young—early twenties—and spent his days in a dark, cheap, rented room containing one shaky table on which was a copy of *Das Kapital*, a hairbrush, Hölderlin's poems and a sandwich, arranged in a picturesque still life. He did not like it when I came to visit him, for he was ashamed of his acquaintance with me before the Socialist and Communist workers with whom I found him engaged in endless discussions. *Weltschmerz*, Russian literature and extremely Left political ideas were the fare on which he lived. But he was young enough to forget these ideals for hours when, beautiful as a young god, he amazed the Berlin salons in the evening. He was a young genius, sensitive and irritable, and no one found it easy to get along with him. Nevertheless we were for years attached to each other in a tense, often endangered, but always steadfast friendship.

. . . He returned in 1939. China had worked miracles on him, as on so many others. His conceptions were clearer, his outlook more harmonious. His political views, aside from the principal one of rejection of Nazism, differed from ours to some extent. He believed that the gulf between England and Germany could be bridged by negotiation without removing the Nazi regime— perhaps his estimate was more correct than ours at the time, but he was certainly wrong in believing that the Nazis could be made to listen to reason. His thorough knowledge of personalities in England and America, his studies of Far Eastern problems, but most of all his ability to win at once the sympathy of foreigners, gradually made him indispensable for our plans.

An equally important Kreisau Circle member escaped execution by a hair's breadth. Theodor Steltzer, a native of Holstein, finished his studies at Göttingen and Munich and entered the army before World War I, in which he served as an officer on General Groener's transport staff. During the chaotic postwar years he came to the conclusion that any true reconstruction of Germany would have to start from the bottom, not the top. His appointment as Landrat, District Administrative Head, at Rendsburg gave him an opportunity to establish *Volkshochschulen,* schools for adult education, throughout his district.

In 1933 the Nazis found an indictment of themselves which Steltzer had written. He was removed from office and arrested on the charge of high treason, but was released without being tried. By 1935 Steltzer had become active in the ecumenical movement and intimate with Moltke, whom he had first met while the latter was attending lectures at the Rendsburg *Volkshochschule*. Moltke introduced him to the Kreisau Circle.

When war broke out Steltzer went back into the army, got in touch with Canaris and in 1940 was sent to Norway as chief of the army transport. He established contact with the Resistance in Norway and often went straight from meetings with General von Falkenhorst, the German military governor, to discussions with the Norwegian underground. He contributed materially to protecting the outstanding Norwegian hero, Bishop Berggrav. When I was checking in Berlin on the Germans whose advice might be useful to Allied Military Government, I received an affidavit from Bishop Berggrav confirming that he and others of the Norwegian underground owe their lives to Theodor Steltzer.

Steltzer returned to Berlin from Norway ten days after July 20 and was arrested at the Tempelhof airport. His name had been found on a list of the members of Goerdeler's proposed coalition government. He was tried by Freisler, together with Moltke and several others of the Kreisau Circle, in January, 1945. Fortunately, two Norwegians he had befriended and who had escaped from the Gestapo to Sweden heard that Steltzer was soon to be executed. Seeking for channels to the top Nazis, they found a Finnish doctor in Stockholm who had treated Himmler. The doctor sent his secretary, a German woman, with a message to his notorious patient. Her car was destroyed by Allied bombers on the trip from Berlin to SS headquarters at Prentzlau, but she finally got a message through the day before Steltzer was to be hanged. By that time Himmler was making his own plans to desert the sinking Nazi ship. "One more or less does not matter now," he remarked, and the date of Steltzer's execution was put off. But he was by no means out of danger. In those last days the Gestapo was liquidating the survivors of July 20 with feverish haste. Steltzer recounts that on April 22 he and eight other men condemned to death were in a shelter in Berlin. The Russians were near the outskirts of the city. Seven of the eight were taken out and shot at the Lehrter railway station, where the Nazis were staging mass executions.

Steltzer is undoubtedly one of the most important of the very few survivors of the anti-Nazi conspiracy, and the only one to assume in postwar Germany the place foreseen for him under the conspirators' program, namely to be the administrative head of the province of Schleswig-Holstein, a post he held under British Military Government.

Only certain members of the Kreisau Circle took a direct part in the various plots to kill Hitler. A majority of the Circle originally opposed resort to assassination and a coup d'état. They felt that the virus of Nazism had permeated the body politic of Germany so deeply that the removal of the leaders would not in itself suffice. Also, they feared a "stab in the back" legend, a myth that some day could fertilize a rebirth of Nazism. They were particularly apprehensive about this in the early years of the war when defeat was not yet apparent to the German people. But when Allied bombs began devastating Germany, more and more recruits were won to the tactic of assassination, and by July 20, 1944, almost every member realized that unless Hitler were physically destroyed Germany would be.

The Kreisau Circle accepted the premise that Germany would lose the war, and that with defeat and the disappearance of National Socialism Germany would be a political and spiritual vacuum. Their primary purpose was to fill this vacuum, to work out the political, intellectual, and spiritual structure for a post-Nazi Germany. They gathered together experts in various administrative fields, trade unionists and churchmen, and to protect themselves from the Gestapo they used the camouflage of planning civilian defense measures in the event of enemy penetration of Germany. This was in line with the duties of several of the Abwehr members of the Kreisau Circle, and gave them access to valuable government statistical material.

In addition to this and to the cover provided by the Abwehr and the Foreign Office, one of Moltke's friends was Edward Waetjen, a Berlin lawyer whose contact with me in Switzerland I describe later. Waetjen had certain Gestapo connections and was often able to warn the Kreisau Circle whenever the actions of any of its members aroused the suspicions of the Nazis' political police.

The Kreisau Circle's program for Germany, set forth in several documents which survived, has far more than an academic interest, even today. This interest does not derive merely from a sentimental respect for the sacrifice of so many of its authors, nor from the fact that their ideas were so largely incorporated in the ideology of the Beck-Goerdeler conspiracy. The Kreisau program represents the way this group of *anti-Nazi Germans* thought Germany could be redeemed from totalitarian imperialism and saved from chaos. The program is also an example of how both Right and Left *can* compromise, and of the result when they do.

The common denominator of the socially divergent Moltke group was the belief in Christian ethics shared by its members. In Christianity they found the answer to the desperate need for ethical values which could guide men in such catastrophic times. Here, these men came to see, was the force that could sustain men in resisting the totalitarian demands of the state, as Peter Yorck so boldly told Judge Freisler.

The Christianity of the Kreisau Circle was not dogmatic or sectarian. It was the simple recognition that man's conduct in Western civilization should be guided by the Sermon on the Mount. This insistence on the spirit rather than the letter of Christianity is affirmed in the writings of the group with a force and simplicity found in few professions of faith in recent times. It is perhaps not too much to say that a Christian revival was the dominant force of the political opposition which saw in Hitler nothing less than the Anti-Christ.

Christian ethics, the Kreisau Circle believed, could be combined with an economic system that would foster prosperity and eliminate the power of the antidemocratic forces in German national life. To this end it seemed to them necessary that the natural wealth of the nation should serve the entire people and that the influence and responsibility of organized labor be strengthened. In short, the economic and political program worked out in great detail by the Kreisau Circle was a Christian socialism.

This Christian socialism entailed the nationalization of heavy industry, banks and insurance companies, and provided that labor should share equally with management in the conduct of industry, even of that part of industry that was to be left for private enterprise. Labor was also to have equal representation in an economic and in an agricultural council that would guide the economy of the nation.

The centralization inherent in even a partial socialization was to be tempered by a political decentralization. Germany was to be divided into provinces of three to five million inhabitants. The boundaries of these provinces roughly coincided with the existing military districts rather than with the old German states, which were extremely unequal in population and economic resources. The provinces were to be united in a federation in which Prussia would not be dominant.

The franchise was given to everyone over twenty-one, and the head of a household had an extra vote for each child under twenty-one. Voting was by secret ballot but only local officials and the members of the provincial diets were to be elected by the people. The provincial diet would elect the provincial *Landesverweser*, or president, and the members of the national Reichstag, which in turn would elect the Reich President. A Reichsrat, or upper chamber of the Reichstag, was to be revived, and its members would consist of the Reich President, the provincial presidents, the chiefs of the economic and agricultural councils and appointees by the Reich President. It should be noted the Kreisau Circle did not feel that Germany was ready for a thoroughgoing democracy. The local assemblies were directly subject to the popular will, but above them persons designated by people's representatives and executive appointees were to control.

Elementary education was to be largely in the hands of the churches. Professional schools and the universities were to be separate. The latter were to devote themselves to non-specialized curricula and the promotion of pure science and the humanities. Administrative posts above a certain level in the provincial and national governments would be open only to graduates of a university *and* an appropriate professional school.

The foreign policy of the Kreisau Circle was based on an acceptance of the Soviet Union into the family of nations and on the ultimate federation of Europe in a commonwealth not unlike the British Empire. National sovereignty was to be limited and a new international order was to be the basis for peace. Germany's permanent strategy of playing the East and the West against each other was to be abandoned. The German army was to be abolished. As for the punishment of Germans for the war and crimes against humanity, the Circle favored trials for war criminals before the Court of International Justice at The Hague. This court, however, was to be changed to include three judges from the victorious nations, two judges of neutral nations, and one judge from the defeated nation. The power to indict was to repose in the nation whose interest had been violated. Who should be considered criminals, the Circle thought, could best be determined in the manner of the English in 1689 as described by Macaulay:

> The rule by which a prince ought after a rebellion to be guided in selecting rebels for punishment is perfectly obvious. The ringleaders, the men of rank, fortune and education, whose power and whose artifices have led the multitude into error, are the proper objects of severity. The deluded population, when once the slaughter on the field of battle is over, can scarcely be treated too leniently.

This, in outline, was the program which the Kreisau Circle believed would, "after Hitler," guide the German people "on the road to individual freedom, to peace, and to decency."

8. The Left

In his midnight broadcast on July 20 Hitler described the attempt to assassinate him as the work of a small clique of ambitious, unscrupulous officers. The world long accepted his judgment of it, but as usual Hitler was lying. The Left was also in the plot.

When I was in Switzerland working with the underground in Germany and in German-occupied Europe, I relied heavily on members of the Social Democratic party and on other Socialists and trade unionists. Among the latter the International Transport Workers Union was particularly effective. I found in these groups devoted men and women willing to risk their lives for the restoration of liberty in Europe. No class worked more vigorously than they to protect the individual against the Nazis, and to try to atone for the ineffectiveness and political mistakes of the Left in the pre-Hitler days.

The Social Democratic party in Germany had lost many members to the Communist party in the years just preceding 1933, and came to regard the Communists as its most dangerous rival. The Communists reciprocated in kind and refused to work with the Social Democrats against the Nazis. In fact, Communists and Nazis, from 1931 on, joined in undermining the cabinet of the Socialist Prussian Minister-President, Otto Braun. Nazis and Communists also collaborated during a strike of the Berlin transportation workers in the autumn of 1932. Communists, as well as Nazis, promoted the feeling of frustration that helped bring Hitler to power, for both had a hatred of the Weimar Republic and a desire for a totalitarian state. If German Socialists today are more vigorous than Socialists elsewhere in refusing to merge with the Communists, it is not because they reject working class unity as such, but rather because the German Socialists, more keenly than other Socialists, have experienced the meaning of totalitarianism.

By the time the Nazis seized power the backbone of the Social Democratic party was already broken. In a series of blatantly unconstitutional maneuvers Papen ousted Social Democrats from the Prussian administration in June, 1932. They did not even try to fight. What a Papen could do in Prussia, Hitler speedily did throughout Germany. Soon after the 1933 elections the Social Democratic party was dissolved by Nazi decree and thousands of Socialists and trade unionists joined the Communists in what soon became the notorious concentration camps of the Nazis. The German Communist party had preceded the Socialists into oblivion. The Göring-planned Reichstag fire was the excuse for outlawing the Communist party and arresting its leaders.*

How little the Communists in Germany were actually prepared for Nazism, and how wrongly they gauged its real nature, is indicated by the fact that the party secretary, Ernst Torgler, surrendered himself voluntarily in order to clear himself and his party of the press allegations that Communists set the Reichstag on fire. Torgler acted as though he believed a Communist might find justice under Hitler.

The imprisonment of their leaders left the Communists without direction and resulted in the disintegration of the German Communist party. The Comintern in Moscow was

* In an affidavit sworn to by General Halder at Nürnberg, Halder stated that in the course of a birthday dinner for the Führer in 1942 "Göring shouted into the conversation, 'The only one who really knows the Reichstag is I, because I put the fire to it.' With that he took the flat of his hand and slapped his thighs."

then following the line that the Nazi dictatorship would soon run itself to death, and leave behind a disrupted society, a bankrupt capitalism, and a weakened and impoverished state. But by 1934 Moscow realized Hitler was not quite so ephemeral. The orders to remain in Germany previously given to the key Communists were reversed. Quite a few made their way to Russia. As for the rank and file, the election returns of March, 1933, the first and last election of the Hitler regime, indicated that even a year before Moscow changed its orders, over a million voters had forsaken the Communists for the Nazis. Thereafter many Communists joined the Nazi party and even became members of the Gestapo. While some did this under party orders, others boxed the political compass and became believers in Nazism. When Stalin made his pact with Hitler in August, 1939, the organized Communist underground in Germany came to a complete standstill. Many who till then had remained steadfast and loyal deserted the party.

It was not until Russia was invaded that the Communist underground revived and obtained support from the outside. The Communist leaders who had gone to Russia organized some assistance for their comrades in Germany, and after Stalingrad formed the Free Germany Committee in Moscow. Some of them, Wilhelm Pieck, Walter Ulbricht and Erwin Hoernle, returned to the Russian zone of Germany immediately after the German surrender. Two others, Hans Neumann and Ernst Remmele, once prominent members of the Reichstag, disagreed with their hosts in Moscow and have not been heard from.

During the war Communist activity in Germany consisted chiefly in smuggling in or printing propaganda material, and distributing it. It was slipped under doors, it was put into letter boxes, it filtered down from balloons exploded in midair by a time fuse. All this was on a relatively limited scale. Toward the end of the war the Communists promoted here and there sabotage of shipyards and transport and some slow-downs in factories. The Communists also incited foreign workers in Germany to revolt. Many plots discovered by the Gestapo in the last months of the war involved foreign workers, and there was at least one attempt to arm and organize them on a large scale known as *Europäische Aktion*.

I do not know of any Communist plots to assassinate Hitler, though several Communists were executed for participation in the July 20 putsch. Toward the end of the war this, of course, was the stock accusation the Nazis made against everyone they wanted to get rid of. The absence of Communist attempts to assassinate leading Nazis may be due in part to the Marxist prohibition against "individual terror," in part to the slender resources available to the Communists so long as they did not join other anti-Nazi groups.

There was, however, one interesting plot in 1943 called *Rote Kapelle,* or Red Chapel, which originally had a political anti-Nazi tinge, and later turned into an organization to provide intelligence for the Red Army.

The leading spirit in *Rote Kapelle* was a Lieutenant Harold Schulze-Boysen, who had been in politics since 1932, when he formed a small political party called *Gegner* (Opposition). At first he opposed both Nazis and Communists—the former he considered too bourgeois, the latter too bureaucratic. He concocted a political farrago around the idea that there was no Left or Right, that political parties did not form a straight line but an incomplete circle, which did not quite close. The Communists and Nazis, of course, were at the unclosed ends of the circle. Schulze-Boysen decided his party would fill that gap and close the circle. He was young, blond, Nordic—a product of the German Youth movement. Always wearing a black sweater, he went around with revolutionaries, surrealists and the rag-tag and bobtail of the "lost generation." He had had trouble with the Nazis early in his career, and only protection in high places—his father was an admiral and his mother a friend of Göring—saved him. Finally, his mother, through Göring's influence, found a place for him in the Air Ministry.

The Russians had seen the possibility of using him, and after Hitler attacked them Schulze-Boysen became one of their important agents in Germany. He had leads not only into the Air Ministry but also to the Foreign Office (through a certain Dolf von Scheliha) and to other important offices through Government Councilor Otto Harnack. The latter had worked closely with the Soviet Embassy during the days of the Hitler-Stalin pact and at that time had received from the Russians his instructions, radio sets and secret codes. *Rote Kapelle* ended when one of the Russian agents, parachuted into Germany, sold out to the Gestapo. Seventy-eight were executed. "It seems a habit in Europe that spiritual seeds be drenched in blood," Schulze-Boysen wrote his parents just before his execution. He became a posthumous hero in the Russian zone of Berlin where a play about *Rote Kapelle* by Günther Weisenborn, one of the participants who survives, had considerable vogue.

From time to time during the war various efforts were made to coordinate Communist underground activity with that of the other left wing parties. In some communities a measure of cooperation was achieved, but on a national scale it was not successful. Just as the Communists had penetrated the Gestapo, so the Gestapo had infiltrated into the Communist underground and there were numerous instances where Socialists, after establishing contact with the Communists, were denounced. And the Communists were not inclined to cooperate. When attempts were made to draw them into the conspiracy to assassinate Hitler they expressed skepticism of the motives of a group that included conservatives and generals. Their skepticism was increased by the developments in Italy after the fall of Mussolini, for they considered Badoglio no less reactionary than the Fascists.

The Social Democrats had sent their most prominent leaders into exile shortly after Hitler became Chancellor. Among them were Rudolf Breitscheid and Rudolf Hilferding. I had known them well, when I was in Berlin in 1920, as the two leading personalities in the left wing of the Social Democratic party of the early Weimar days. Both were arrested in southern France in 1941 and delivered up to the Gestapo by Vichy. Hilferding committed suicide in his Paris cell; Breitscheid died in Buchenwald.

Another prominent exiled Socialist leader was Wilhelm Hoegner. A Bavarian and former member of the Reichstag and the Bavarian Landtag, he had been on the Landtag commission that wrote the scathing report on Hitler's bizarre beer hall putsch of 1923 and had at that time helped to send Hitler to jail. Hoegner was fortunate enough to thwart Hitler's revenge in 1933 by escaping, first to Austria, and then to Switzerland, where he became one of the leaders-in-exile of the Socialist underground in Germany. He was a constant source of help to me in establishing contact with members of the German Left in Switzerland. Returning to Bavaria as soon as our armies had occupied it, he soon became the head of the Bavarian government.

These and other Socialist exiles succeeded in organizing, before war began, outside support for work within Germany, which was entrusted to tested but less conspicuous leaders, who pretended to sever all connections with the Second (Socialist) International. The wisdom of this tactic was proved when Hitler outlawed the party and underground work had to be organized. The 85-year-old Social Democratic party had been underground before—Bismarck had outlawed it for eleven years—and could count on a large number of trained and disciplined members to build undercover units throughout the country.

In the summer of 1933 the party's executive committee, in exile at Prague, organized the SOPADE (abbreviation for

Socialist Party of Germany), a network of so-called "border secretariats" which, from Czechoslovakia, Switzerland, France, Belgium, the Netherlands, and Denmark maintained contact with the party in Germany. It supplied money, machinery for clandestine printing, information, guidance and assistance for the families of imprisoned party members. It also smuggled out of Germany endangered party members and Jews, as well as political and economic intelligence. Until Munich the SOPADE maintained a highly efficient information service which supplied the outside world with much of the reliable data that came out of Nazi Germany. The "Green Reports," as they were called, were printed first in Prague and later in London and had a wide distribution which included the foreign offices of many governments.

After Munich SOPADE was forced to cease operations from Prague and transferred its headquarters to Paris, and with the Nazi occupation of virtually all Europe its activities were drastically curtailed. The International Transport Workers Union assumed some of SOPADE's work, especially the publication of the "Green Reports." Cooperating with the underground Socialist cells was a group of former Communist intellectuals called "New Beginning"; a remnant of the former Socialist Workers Party (SAP); and a third wing made up former Socialist Militants (Internationaler Sozialistischer Kampfbund, or ISK).

Splits within Socialist parties have been their great weakness. There was a split within SOPADE—and it was reflected in splits inside Germany. It fell to the lot of two of the younger Socialist leaders to try to restore harmony: Carlo Mierendorff and Theodor Haubach.

Carlo Mierendorff had been editor of the Socialist newspaper *Volksfreund* in Darmstadt and a member of the Reichstag until 1933. A close friend of his, the German playwright Carl Zuckmayer, describes Mierendorff as a citizen of the world who "studied, wrote, worked, laughed, slaved, fought, drank and loved through many a German landscape, village and town. One could hardly imagine a more impulsive and at the same time active, tense and purposeful life." The Nazis hated him, said Zuckmayer, "for he possessed what they could never have, intimacy with the people." He was, of all the Socialists, their most dangerous enemy. From the spring of 1933 until the winter of 1937 Mierendorff was in a concentration camp. Upon his release he joined with Theodor Haubach in clandestine anti-Nazi activity and was killed in an Allied bombing raid on Leipzig in December, 1943.

Mierendorff and Haubach had been fellow students at Heidelberg. In 1924 Haubach became one of the co-founders of the Reichsbanner, an organization which aimed at promoting the republican idea. Later, when the Nazi Storm Troopers became troublesome, the Reichsbanner developed into a sort of republican militia, pledged to uphold the Weimar Constitution and defend the government against both Communists and Nazis. Haubach had been editor in chief of the Social Democratic newspaper, *Hamburger Echo;* later he became chief of the press office in the Reich Ministry of the Interior, and then public relations man in the Berlin Police Department. He, too, served a term in a concentration camp.

Mierendorff and Haubach in time became the de facto leaders of the Socialist underground. Karl Gruber, for example, during the war an "exile" in Berlin, and later Foreign Minister of a freed Austria, told me that he started his underground work with them.

The Socialists realized they alone could not make the plans for a post-Hitler Germany and that the efforts of all oppositional groups would have to be coordinated if a workable program was to be evolved. As the war dragged on the Socialist leaders drew together and the Moltke circle at Kreisau became the chief forum for their discussions. Mierendorff, Haubach, Ludwig Schwamb, Adolf Reichwein, and other concentration camp alumni participated, not only as individuals, but also as representatives of the Socialist underground.

As another step in building up a united Left front, the Socialists made common cause with trade unionists who had established underground cells throughout the country after the Nazis destroyed the German trade unions. Their leader was Wilhelm Leuschner, who ultimately became the Left's chief representative in the political coalition built up in preparation for July 20.

Leuschner, a wood sculptor by profession, enjoyed the political maneuvering into which he was plunged almost as soon as he got into the trade union movement. He was on the Darmstadt city council, in the Hessian Diet from 1918 to 1933, and for a while was Minister of Interior of Hesse. In 1932 he was deputy head of the Free German Trade Unions, which had four and a half million members. In his last letter to his son, written a few days before his execution on September 29, 1944, Leuschner wrote: "Keep united, build up again." And a fellow prisoner in the Ravensbrück concentration camp reported that Leuschner communicated one word to him in sign language as he walked to the gallows: "Unity." How poignantly Leuschner must then have realized that disunity among the anti-Nazi forces had helped to open the door to Hitler.

Leuschner had recognized the dangerous character of the Nazi movement earlier than most trade union leaders. When Papen made the first move against the Left in 1932, Leuschner, as Minister of the Interior of Hesse, controlled the police and mobilized it when Nazi Storm Troopers threatened to take over.

Naturally, Leuschner was a marked man after the Nazis came in and raided and closed the trade union headquarters in Berlin's Wallstrasse. Nevertheless, he insisted on going to Geneva to represent German labor at the International Labor Office. While there the notorious Dr. Robert Ley, recognizing Leuschner's great popularity, asked him to co-operate in the Nazi Labor Front, into which the Nazis forced the membership of the liquidated trade unions. Leuschner declined, and despite warnings of what would happen to him, he returned to Germany. Ley had probably learned that one of the purposes of Leuschner's Geneva visit was to prevent the ILO from recognizing the Nazi Labor Front. Hardly had Leuschner crossed the German frontier before he was arrested. He was put in a concentration camp, but his connections with the ILO made it embarrassing for Hitler to keep him imprisoned. He was released in 1935 and for a time thereafter lived in disguise in a small pension on the Kurfürstendamm in Berlin under the assumed name of Dr. Wiese.

Leuschner then established a small factory in Berlin for the manufacture of a new device for filling beer glasses at bars, invented by a union colleague, Ernst Schneppenhorst. The factory, whose employees were almost exclusively Socialists and former union members, became the headquarters of the trade union underground. Its "salesmen," before the war, traveled abroad and maintained contact with international trade unions. Leuschner, Schneppenhorst and others traveled throughout Germany ostensibly to sell beer gadgets; in reality to contact former comrades and organize them in secret cells.

Through his friend General von Hammerstein and independent "business contacts" with the military (which suddenly showed an interest in beer faucets) Leuschner came into contact with the generals of the opposition. General Beck, disguised by blue glasses, was a frequent visitor at the factory. Abwehr men occasionally dropped in. Even the conservative Canaris, who had formerly dealt with such Socialists as the former ministers of the Weimar period Karl Severing and Paul Loebe, turned to Leuschner.

Cooperation with the predominantly Catholic Christian Trade Unions was effected through its foremost representative, Jakob Kaiser, who was very close to General von Hammerstein. When the Nazis liquidated the Christian Trade Unions they tried to get Kaiser to sign a statement that the unions had voluntarily dissolved themselves. He refused and went underground in the Rhineland. After July 20, Kaiser took refuge in the Berlin home of an inconspicuous school teacher and stayed there until the Russians occupied the city. Later he became the leader of the Christian Democratic Union in the Russian zone.

In their earlier underground years the trade unions considered a general strike a possibility. Sabotage, small acts of violence, a general strike and finally open rebellion was the program they would have liked to follow. Leuschner made preparations for a railroad strike in 1938. But lethargy and the Gestapo were too strong. The Nazi Labor Front had its own spy organization with agents in every factory to keep watch on former trade union members.

Another Socialist who had an important part in the conspiracy was Dr. Julius Leber, whom Judge Freisler, during Leber's trial, called "the Lenin of the German working class movement." Originally a business man, a naval officer in World War I, he became editor of the Lübeck newspaper *Volksbote,* and in 1924 was a Socialist deputy in the Reichstag. The Nazis put him in a concentration camp. He was released after several years, went underground in Lübeck, after an adequate interval returned to Berlin and camouflaged his clandestine activities behind a small coal business, "Mayer und Nachfolger." Leber was a brilliant man, but a bit too rash for the role of conspirator. His last-minute attempt to bring the Communists into the plot shortly before July 20 ended disastrously. Leber worked closely with Trott and Stauffenberg, and was the best source the conspirators had regarding the attitude of the German workers. He was also one of the links between the conspirators and the Kreisau group.

The idea of "revolution from the top" is always disquieting to the Left. But by 1942 Socialists realized general strikes and mass uprisings were impossible, that the help of the army was indispensable, and that Beck and Goerdeler were necessary if such help was to be obtained. They hoped to replace an eventual Beck-Goerdeler government with one more to their liking and more to the Left. Mierendorff told Professor Alfred Weber in Heidelberg: "We are obliged to act without the masses and must leave the initiative to the generals." However, the Socialists and trade unionists secured promises of important positions in the proposed revolutionary government. Leuschner, Leber and Haubach were all to have cabinet posts.

Gustav Dahrendorf, one of the important Social Democratic survivors, summed up the position of the left wing participants in the plot: all political objectives had to be subordinated to the task of doing away with the Nazis. "We had one aim: to put an end to Fascism, to put an end to war."

9. Church and University

"If a crisis should arise for this National Socialist state the churches and the ministers would pass from concealed to open opposition." These are the words of Hitler's deputy, Martin Bormann, in a secret report sent to the German High Command just before the outbreak of war in 1939. The evidence bears Bormann out.

By flouting the ethics of Christianity and the fundamental Christian concept of the dignity of man, Hitler helped to knit the forces of the opposition. Men as different as a Canaris and a Niemöller, as divergent as militant leaders of labor on the one hand, and military men like Hammerstein and Beck on the other, were brought together in a common cause.

Such recognition as there was in Germany of the barbarity of the Nazi regime was largely in Christian circles. In 1942 Moltke wrote that the backbone of the spiritual awakening against Nazism was in the Protestant and Catholic churches and it was on this foundation that the opposition was trying to build. "Today," he added, "it is beginning to dawn on a not too numerous but active part of the population not that they have been misled, not that they are in for a hard time, not that they might lose the war, but that what is done is sinful," and that as Christians they were personally responsible for every savage act.

Hitler absorbed into his totalitarian state, neutralized or suppressed every organization except the churches. Nazi records reveal that the best Hitler hoped to achieve was a sort of modus vivendi with religion, a truce based on the cynical Nazi theory that Hitler would let the churches take care of the "hereafter" if they would leave the present to him.

But the gulf between Christianity and the National Socialist way of life could never be bridged, and the more intelligent Nazis realized it. Among the Nürnberg documents there are many letters on this subject from Bormann to Alfred Rosenberg, the Nazi theoretician and author of one of the important texts of Nazi ideology, *The Myth of the Twentieth Century,* which the Catholic Church put on the Index. "Christianity and National Socialism," Bormann wrote, "differ so fundamentally that it will not be possible to construct a Christian teaching which will be completely compatible with the point of view of National Socialism." And he added: "The churches cannot be conquered by a compromise between National Socialism and Christian teachings but only through a new ideology." Bormann's letters reveal considerable impatience with the attempts of the notorious Dr. Kerrl, Reich minister for the churches, to reconcile Christian and Nazi teachings. He was equally impatient with Rosenberg for his failure to find an ideology capable of replacing Christianity. "I would think that today," he wrote him in 1940, "seven years after taking over the power, it should be possible to set up principles for a National Socialist conduct of life."

The Nazis never solved this problem; *Mein Kampf* could not replace the Sermon on the Mount.

In view of the numerical strength and ancient traditions of the German churches, both Protestant and Catholic, and Hitler's failure to complete his domination of them, it is surprising that they were not a greater danger to him than they proved to be. Unfortunately the churches were slow to realize that Nazism was not merely a "political change" but an attack on basic Christian principles—almost as slow as the German people were to recognize its threat to their freedom and as foreign countries were to recognize the menace to their peace. Bound to neutrality in temporal matters and the avoidance of conflicts with "Caesar," a cherished church tradition supported by Scripture, the churches, for a considerable time, were the victims of self-deception as well as of Hitler's cunning. After the Gestapo state was thoroughly organized, the churches, with certain notable exceptions, were relegated to the role of passive resistance.

It must be remembered that the anti-Christian character of Nazism was not accentuated in the days of free elections when Hitler needed votes. Moreover, in both Protestant and Catholic churches there were men who believed nationalism was a weapon against Communism and Marxist materialism. And in the bemused mind of the lower middle class, which made up the bulk of churchgoers, the Weimar Republic was responsible for the inflation and the ensuing economic miseries, and for the decay of morals following the first war. Aristocratic and upper middle class Christians, and many among the clergy of both confessions, believed Hitler would end political strife and effect economic recovery. They deluded themselves into accepting at face value the Nazi party's claim that it stood for "a positive Christianity."

When Adolf Hitler and the aged President von Hindenburg rode together to the historic Garrison Church in Potsdam to invoke God's blessing upon the new Reich, a majority of German churchgoers felt assured. Hitler's "pious" utterances and Hindenburg's well known religious attitude comforted the Protestants; Papen's presence in the government reassured the Catholics. Such naïveté may seem unbelievable today. But in Hitler's initial cabinet only three of twelve ministers were Nazis: Adolf Hitler, Wilhelm Frick (Interior), and Hermann Göring (at first minister without portfolio). In other words, only one important post, except for the Chancellor, was in Nazi hands. Franz von Papen was the Vice-Chancellor and Reich Commissar for the Prussian State. The other ministers were Konstantin von Neurath, Foreign Affairs; Alfred Hugenberg, Economics; Lutz Count Schwerin von Krosigk, Finance; Franz Gürtner, Justice; Paul von Eltz-Rübenach, Postoffice and Traffic; Franz Seldte, Labor; General Werner von Blomberg, War; and Hjalmar Schacht, President of the Reichsbank and as such member of the cabinet.

Only one of these men showed real concern for Christianity. Eltz, in January, 1937, refused the party emblem, wrote Hitler that his conscience and his belief in the principles of Christianity made it impossible for him to accept party membership, and that he could no longer tolerate the party's attacks upon the Christian faith. And he resigned. The other aging and reactionary members of that first cabinet—except for the spasmodic opposition after 1938 of the vain and mercurial Schacht—served the Führer until they died, were discarded, or were caught by the Allies.

The (Catholic) Center Party at first believed it could play under Hitler its role of 1919 when it entered a coalition with Social Democrats in order to defeat the militant and revolutionary Left. The Center, early in 1933, voted for the "Enabling Act" which gave Hitler's cabinet full powers in the hope, apparently, that the non-Nazi majority in the cabinet would serve as a better brake on Hitler than the Nazi-dominated Reichstag. Hitler's ostensible eagerness to effect an agreement with the Pope also helped to keep the Center party in line. But the Concordat signed by Papen on July 20, 1933, the first real political success of Hitler's government (it included a revocation of the Church's previous prohibition against Catholics joining the Nazi party), was really the signal for the beginning of Nazi pressure on the Catholic Church. Center Party officials were thrown out of office and the party was dissolved in December, 1933. Catholic youth organizations were largely incorporated in the Hitler Youth.

The Protestants fared similarly. Hitler made great promises to them while campaigning for power, and assured Protestant leaders that the anti-religious utterances of prominent Nazis were merely individual opinions and that Germany would continue to be a Christian state. The Nazis no sooner had power than they "unified" the various Protestant denominations under their stooge, Reich Bishop Müller, nicknamed "Lügen Müller" (lying Muller), a stupid army chaplain, and maneuvered the Evangelical Youth into the Hitler Youth. It was to combat Müller's "German Christian" movement that Pastor Niemöller and Bishop Wurm, the Protestant Bishop of Württemberg, and others organized a Protestant revivalism known as "the Confessional Church." This gave the active anti-Nazi Protestants a vehicle through which they could register a protest against the anti-Christian Hitler state.

In both the Protestant and Catholic churches there was some hesitation over the proper course to pursue under Hitler. Each had its quota of ambitious men who had lost their hold on a firm Christian faith, were lured by temporal power and went along with the Nazis. On the Protestant side such men helped Hitler to organize his "German Christian" church, which flourished particularly in Thuringia, where some of the worst Nazis were members. Some Protestant pastors were weak and convinced themselves their duty was only to preach Christianity and that they could leave to their flocks the task of drawing conclusions as to the practical application of their sermons in the Nazi state. Others, and there were honest men among them, thought it pointless to expose their parishioners to the concentration camp, and felt they should stay with their congregations and lead them as best they could without attacking state policy. But there was a third group of men in both churches who felt they must combat Nazism, whatever the risks. In the Protestant Church there were many who followed the example of

Niemöller and Bishop Wurm, and who, like Niemöller, were put in concentration camps.

The Catholic parish clergy suffered as much as the Protestant pastors, but the higher Catholic hierarchy occupied a slightly more favorable position than the corresponding Protestant ecclesiastics inasmuch as Hitler never wanted a complete break with the Vatican. On one occasion the Bishop of Breslau publicly prayed that he might be sent to a concentration camp. Hitler then gave orders that bishops should be unmolested and thus "have no opportunity to become martyrs."

The Bishop of Münster (Count von Galen, who was made a Cardinal after the war and died in March, 1946) was one of the earliest and most courageous Catholic opponents of Nazism. His sermons were often read aloud in other churches, sent in chain letters all over Germany, and reproduced in Allied broadcasts. The Nazis could not decide what to do about him. He was the subject of endless conferences, and their dilemma is epitomized in a report of one of Goebbels's assistants (Walter Tiessler) to Martin Bormann, regarding a suggestion that Galen be *hanged:*

. . . this measure can be decided only by the Führer himself. He [Goebbels] fears, however, that the population of Münster would have to be written off for the duration of the war if anything were done against the Bishop. And one might as well add all of Westphalia. . . . He maintains the point of view that it would be better to keep up pretenses toward the church for the duration of the war. One can attack an opponent only when one is actually in a position to meet his counterattack. But it is very difficult to counterattack the church during wartime, perhaps it is impossible. . . . After the war the Führer should announce, together with his great social measures, that the entire property of the church belongs to the German people from now on. In the joy over the victory and the social reconstruction, it would be childishly easy to carry out this proposal.

Goebbels' opinion did not prevail, and the Nazis continued throughout the war to do what they could to bring the church to heel. Church processions were forbidden because they would "wear out shoe leather." Recalcitrant pastors were called up for military service (pastors with churches were not exempted from military service until General Olbricht, one of the conspirators, ordered them to be in January, 1944). Witnesses were bribed to testify that a particular priest or pastor was a homosexual, dealt in foreign exchange, or had stolen church funds. Seminaries were closed —usually on the pretext that they were hotbeds of immorality. And though German boys and girls were still told the story of the miracle of the loaves and fishes, they learned immediately afterward that their Führer had done even greater things—had found food, shelter and work for *millions*.

Bormann wanted to eliminate all religious education. In 1941 he wrote the Gauleiters:

No human being would know anything of Christianity if it had not been drilled into him in his childhood by pastors. The so-called God Almighty in no wise gives any knowledge of his existence to young people in advance, but in an astonishing manner, in spite of his omnipotence, leaves this to the efforts of the pastors. If therefore in the future your youth learns nothing more of Christianity, whose doctrines are far below ours, Christ will disappear automatically.

A story typical of the treatment of Catholics came out during one of Freisler's trials. Major Ludwig von Leonrod, implicated in the attempt of July 20, disclosed in the course of his defense that he had asked an army chaplain who was a priest whether it was a sin to kill a tyrant and the priest had said no. Freisler insisted that the prisoner call the priest to testify in his behalf. When the priest confirmed that the major had asked him a hypothetical question and had received a hypothetical answer, Freisler turned upon the chaplain and declared that he was no longer a witness but on trial for his life. He, too, was hanged.

Neither the Protestant nor the Catholic church, as an institution, was involved in the plot against Hitler. But many churchmen were. Outstanding among them was Pastor Dietrich Bonhoeffer, whose visit to Sweden to inform the Bishop of Chichester of the plans of the conspiracy has been mentioned. Bonhoeffer, the son of the famous psychiatrist, was one of the foremost contemporary Protestant theologians. His attitude, revealed at a secret church meeting in Geneva in 1941, was: "I pray for the defeat of my nation. Only in defeat can we atone for the terrible crimes we have committed against Europe and the world." He became active in the conspiracy, was arrested after July 20, and was only thirty-eight years old when he was killed by drunken SS men in the Flossenbürg concentration camp on April 9, 1945, shortly before American troops reached there.

Dr. Eugen Gerstenmaier, a member of the Kreisau Circle, whom I came to know well, was a prominent layman high in the councils of the Evangelical Church. Like Bonhoeffer, he was convinced that spiritual opposition to Nazism was not enough and that Nazism had to be destroyed if Christianity was to survive in Germany. Before the war he strove to break down the reluctance of many Protestant ministers to commit by word and deed what the Nazis called "treason against the State." After war broke out he organized relief for prisoners of war and for the slave labor the Nazis imported from countries they had overrun. This work enabled him to travel abroad.

To this day he does not understand why, when on July 20 he was arrested in the War Office in the Bendlerstrasse, he was not executed on the spot, as were so many of the other conspirators. He assumes it was because the Gestapo hoped to get from him information about other church leaders. But he knows of no reason why, after a trial, he was sentenced only to seven years' imprisonment at hard labor when others, tried with him, were condemned to death. Gerstenmaier was liberated from the prison in Bayreuth by American troops and immediately became active in relief and reconstruction work in Germany.

From Switzerland during the war years I kept in touch with developments in the German Protestant churches through Dr. Hans Schoenfeld, whose work with the World Council of Churches brought him often to Geneva. He had endeavored for many years to combat the influence of Nazism and to develop relations between the German Evangelical Church and church leaders in Europe and the United States. On the Catholic side I came to know in Switzerland a remarkable figure, the Jesuit Father Friedrich Muckermann. Forced to leave Germany early in the Hitler regime, he continued to write and preach against the Nazis, first from Holland and then from France. Finally he escaped into Switzerland. His publication *Der Deutsche Weg,* which continued to have considerable clandestine circulation in Germany, and his radio broadcasts from France in the early days of the war, were telling indictments of Nazism.

Goerdeler and Moltke ascribed great importance to the collaboration of churchmen. They frequently consulted church leaders, particularly the Protestant bishops of Württemberg, Berlin and Stuttgart, and the Catholic Cardinal von Preysing. They were motivated not only by the desire to have church support for the government they hoped would succeed Hitler, but also by an interest in practical cooperation between the great Christian faiths. Both men realized how the divisions within Christianity worked to the advantage of Hitler, who made the Protestants believe he was about to unleash the final struggle against the Catholic Church, and the Catholics that he was the defender of Rome from Communism.

Some progress was made. Representatives of the Lutheran

and Reformed churches came to realize that their common plight under the Nazis made the theological differences between Luther and Zwingli unimportant. Catholics and Protestants met secretly in the monastery of Ettal and found common ground in their resistance to the Nazi paganism. There is reason to believe that this cooperation born of bitter underground struggle continues as Germany confronts the misery, want, and nihilism that are the Nazi legacy. "A greater understanding than ever before has been developed between Catholic and Protestant leaders," said the Catholic Bishop Hilfrich of Limburg in April, 1946.

It was at Kreisau that much was done to build this Christian collaboration on a non-sectarian basis. Protestants, Catholics and Social Democrats worked in close harmony. When in January, 1945, Count von Moltke was tried—along with Father Delp, the Jesuit from Munich; Eugen Gerstenmaier and Theodor Steltzer, leading Lutherans; and Theodor Haubach, Social Democratic leader—Freisler was particularly infuriated over Moltke's collaboration with the Jesuits. In one of his last letters to his wife * describing the details of his trial Moltke paraphrased Freisler's outburst as follows:

And who was present? A Jesuit father! Of all people, a Jesuit father! And a Protestant minister, and three others who were later condemned to death for complicity in the July 20 plot! And not a single National Socialist! No, not one! Well, all I can say is, now we're really getting the naked truth [literally the German reads "now the fig leaf is down."] A Jesuit father, and

* Count Helmuth von Moltke's letter to his wife, Freya von Moltke, written in the Tegel prison on January 10, 1945, a few days before his execution, was smuggled out by the prison chaplain, Harald Pölchau, who secretly aided many of Hitler's victims. A copy of this letter was kindly given me by Countess Moltke, who shared with her husband the dangers of the anti-Nazi underground. This letter and two other letters of Moltke's, one written in 1942, were published by English friends of Count Moltke in the *Round Table*, June, 1946, and reprinted by the Oxford University Press. The Jesuit father referred to in Freisler's diatribe is Father Delp; the Protestant is undoubtedly Eugen Gerstenmaier, and the Provincial Head of the Jesuits is Fr. Roesch, Father Provincial of the Bavarian Jesuits.

with him, of all people, you discuss the question of civil disobedience! And the Provincial Head of the Jesuits, you knew him too! He even came to Kreisau once! A Provincial of the Jesuits, one of the highest officials of Germany's most dangerous enemies, he visits Count Moltke in Kreisau! And you're not ashamed of it, even though no decent German would touch a Jesuit with a barge-pole! People who have been excluded from all national service, because of their attitude! If I know there's a Provincial of the Jesuits in a town, it's almost enough to keep me out of that town altogether! And the other reverend gentleman! What was he after there? Such people should confine their attentions to the hereafter, and leave us here in peace! And you went visiting Bishops! Looking for something you'd lost, I suppose! Where do you get your orders from? You get your orders from the Führer, and the National Socialist Party! That goes for you as much as for any other German, and anyone who takes his orders, no matter how indirectly, from the agents of the other world, is taking them from the enemy, and will be dealt with accordingly!

The courageous example of Niemöller, Bonhoeffer, Bodelschwingh, Wurm, Galen, Preysing and many others, priests, pastors and laymen united in their Christian faith, helped to create the atmosphere in which a conspiracy against Hitler could grow. Undoubtedly due to such men the churches played a part in the opposition to Hitler. Why they did not do more to undermine the anti-Christian Hitler regime, and why, even in Christian circles, there was vacillation over Nazism in the early days, are questions which the German churches would do well to ponder today.

The German universities must also examine themselves in the light of what they did and did not do under Nazism.

For a variety of reasons the German universities, faculty and students, played a far less important role than the churches in the opposition to Hitler. The Nazi atmosphere was stifling to intellectual life and many outstanding leaders of German thought in the academic field left Germany in the years before the war. The pastor had to stay with his flock but many professors went where they could express their views with the freedom that is essential to true learning. Moreover, the Nazis were able to regiment the universities and their faculties far more than they did the churches. The universities had been hot beds of Hitlerism and militarism even before Hitler came to power and thereafter every university had a large quota of Nazi professors. Often the straight-thinking professors who stayed on in the German universities withdrew from all politics into what some of them now refer to as their "inner emigration."

Wilhelm Furtwängler made himself spokesman for this attitude when he appeared before the denazification court in Berlin. In an impassioned appeal to the tribunal he tried to justify his work in Germany under the Nazis. "Art," he said, "must stand above politics." Those professors and artists who experienced what the Nazi regime did to their professions would be loath to accept Furtwängler's conclusion.

The students were particularly susceptible to the Nazi philosophy. By 1939 they were preponderantly members of the Nazi party or sympathetic to it. There were exceptions, of course, both among faculty and students, and the incident at the University of Munich early in 1943 was the outstanding example of university opposition to the Nazis and their war.

After the German debacle at Stalingrad, when the Russian radio filled the air of Germany with the names and addresses of German troops captured at Stalingrad, in every German town and hamlet there was mounting bitterness and discontent. There were then few able-bodied students left in the universities. The student body in Munich, for example, was composed of girls, cripples and Nazi "student leaders." One day in February, 1943, Gauleiter Giesel of Bavaria addressed the students of the Munich university and declared the women students would better serve the Nazi state by child-bearing than by seeking higher education. The audience shouted him down, overpowered the SS and Gestapo men at the exits, throwing several of them down the stairs, and continued their demonstrations in the streets of Munich.

The 25-year-old student of medicine Hans Scholl, and his sister Sophie, twenty-one years old, a student of biology, decided that this demonstration showed the time was ripe for open agitation against Hitler. Both had fought the Hitler Youth movement in their home town of Ulm, and had been in trouble with the Gestapo. In the university they had gathered around them a small group that sent anonymous letters to intellectuals and professional men throughout the Reich urging them to use their influence, and to organize against the Nazi party. With the help of the venerable Professor Karl Huber, a teacher of philosophy, the Scholls printed and distributed a leaflet containing such slogans as: "Resign from the party formations. . . . Fight the party. . . . The German name is shamed forever if German youth does not rise at last to take revenge. . . . The dead of Stalingrad are calling you. . . . Our people are rising against the enslavement of Europe by National Socialism." Friends in universities at Vienna and Jena also distributed the leaflets.

Finally they became too bold. On February 19, 1943, Hans and Sophie threw hundreds of copies of their leaflet from a balcony at the university. They were seen by the building superintendent, who betrayed them to the Gestapo. Their trial began three days later, and was deemed so important that Freisler himself flew from Berlin to preside. Sophie Scholl had been tortured to such an extent that she appeared in court with a broken leg. But she still held her own with Freisler. "You know as well as we do," she said, "that the war is lost. Why are you so cowardly that you won't admit it?"

That afternoon she and her brother were beheaded. Professor Huber and many others of the "Scholl clique," as the Nazis called it, were executed shortly afterward. The repercussions in Munich were profound and the whole city was moved by the fact that a young girl had dared so much. Today a school in Berlin bears her name.

There was some contact between university faculties and the Beck-Goerdeler conspiracy.

In the fall of 1942, Pastor Bonhoeffer visited Freiburg University and prevailed upon several trusted members of the faculty to prepare a memorandum on the position of the Confessional Church in Europe's reconstruction predicated on the assumption of Germany's defeat. This led to secret meetings between the professors and church leaders and Goerdeler. The resulting manuscript became part of the intellectual armory of the putsch. These professors—Adolf Lampe, Constantin von Dietze, Gerhard Ritter, Walter Eucken, and Erik Wolf—were arrested after July 20, but were liberated when the Russians entered Berlin.

Goerdeler was also assisted by several members of the faculty of Berlin University; in particular, the law professor Rudolf Smend. Smend and Goerdeler were close friends and the former advised the would-be Chancellor on the way to cut through the legalistic tangle the Nazis had thrown up for their own protection—no easy task, as any Military Government officer in Germany can testify.

One of the underground's strangest characters was Albrecht Haushofer, the son of Hitler's famous geopolitician. He was fat, whimsical, sentimental, romantic and unquestionably brilliant. Like his father, he was a geopolitician and had traveled all over the world. He was also the bosom friend of Rudolf Hess, and in the days when he was a Nazi Albrecht Haushofer was on Ribbentrop's staff, and later on Papen's.

He first suspected the good sense of the Nazis when Hitler took over Czechoslovakia. He became certain that

Germany could not conquer the world if Hess's flight to England was any criterion of Nazi acumen. "How can you make politics with such fools?" he asked when he heard of Hess's mad adventure.

Hitler was not at all sure Albrecht was not responsible for Hess's action, and summoned him to Berchtesgaden. He easily cleared himself, but later wrote Hitler that the war would have catastrophic consequences for Germany. He was arrested, but released, probably out of consideration for his father. He then drifted ever closer to the conspiracy and finally was in it heart and soul. After July 20 he tried to get across the Swiss border, but was caught high up in the Bavarian Alps. A few days before Berlin was liberated he and other inmates of the Lehrterstrasse prison who knew too much (Albrecht knew of Himmler's contacts with Popitz, described elsewhere) were murdered by the SS. The Russians found his dead body in the basement of a bombed house near the jail.

Albrecht Haushofer was a typical outgrowth of the German Youth movement which helped to bring on the disaster and was at last itself overwhelmed by it. During his last days in prison he wrote a series of sonnets on rough scraps of paper procured from his jailors. They tell the story of his disillusionment with Nazism and of his break with his father—his father who had "helped let the devil out into the world." But Albrecht realized his own complicity and guilt. His guilt was not that for which the courts had convicted him, but

> Early I saw the misery's whole course—
> I spoke my warning, but not harsh enough nor clear!
> How guilty I have been I now know here. . . .

Haushofer's condemnation of himself applies to many German intellectuals. They too were guilty of the sin of cautious indifference. And most of them were guiltier than Haushofer, for when he belatedly realized what the Nazis had done to Germany he did not continue as a silent onlooker. He risked and lost his life.

10. Contacts in Foreign Countries

I reached Switzerland as the tide of war turned in November of 1942. The battle of El Alamein had been won, the successful defense of Stalingrad was in progress and Allied troops had landed in Africa the day before I crossed the Swiss frontier. I was the last American to reach Switzerland legally before the German invasion of southern France cut the Swiss off completely. Until American troops broke through to the frontier near Geneva in August, 1944, Switzerland was an island of democracy in a sea of Nazi and Fascist despotism. Radio communication was our only link with the outside world.

Switzerland was the only neutral country with a common land frontier with Germany and by all odds the best point from which to observe what was going on in Hitler's Germany. Refugees seeking asylum had fled to Switzerland throughout the seven prewar Hitler years, and a trickle of refugees were able to make their way over the border even after war broke out, though many perished in the attempt. Some of these refugees succeeded, in various underground ways, in maintaining contacts with their friends on the German side of the frontier. They were a fruitful source of information. In addition, German officials and business men who had a legitimate reason to travel were able to come and go with some freedom if they remained in the good books of the Gestapo. A certain number of these double-crossed the Gestapo and were glad enough to talk about conditions in

Germany if they were sure they would not be betrayed. The German press, the German radio and even the German propaganda, when correctly discounted, furnished the background raw material for gauging the situation in Germany. In time, we were able to develop the more daring techniques of sending people back and forth across this dangerous frontier.

One of the first tasks assigned to me from Washington was to find out what I could about any underground anti-Nazi movements in Germany. It was natural that I should start out by making discreet inquiry among the men and women who, for religious, racial or political reasons, had fled into Switzerland. Among them were members of the trade unions, who maintained contact with the persecuted and scattered remnants of the German trade unionism which Hitler had destroyed. There were also prominent church leaders, Protestants and Catholics, who kept in touch with their co-religionists across the frontier.

Various clues finally led me to Hans Bernd Gisevius and through him I was able at a relatively early date to make contact with the conspirators who planned and carried out the July 20 plot.

Gisevius was a descendant of an old family of German civil servants and had entered the Prussian administration when he completed his law examinations in 1933. He was then a member of the German National People's Party and of the Stahlhelm and, though not a Nazi, was considered politically reliable and was attached to the newly formed secret state police, the Gestapo. He had not been more than a few days in his new office when he found that its real purpose was not to arrest those guilty of the worst crimes but to protect them. Perplexed as to what it was all about, he asked one of his colleagues, a professional civil servant: "Tell me, please, am I in a police office, or in a robbers' cave?" The answer was: "You are in a robbers' cave and you will soon see a lot more." Gisevius shortly quarreled with his boss, Rudolf Diels, one of Himmler's predecessors, and moved over to the Ministry of the Interior, under Frick. In the course of time he happened upon Major (later General) Oster, and through him, after an adventurous career, went into the Abwehr.

After the war Gisevius was summoned to the Nürnberg trials by counsel for Dr. Schacht and Dr. Frick, but actually became a witness for the prosecution against Göring, and most of the other defendants except Schacht. At the close of his testimony, which was highly damaging to many of the Nazi criminals, Dr. Seidl, counsel for Hess and Gauleiter Frank, attempted to discredit his testimony.

QUESTION: Witness, during the war were you at any time active in the service of a foreign power?
ANSWER: At no time.

The English president of the tribunal interrupted the examination to ascertain the purpose of the line of questioning. Seidl explained that it related to the credibility of the witness. If he were in the intelligence service of a foreign power that would affect his credibility. Over Mr. Justice Jackson's protest the question was allowed, and Gisevius repeated his answer:

I have said that I was never in the service of a foreign power. I was in the service of a *good* Germany.

The examination continued:

QUESTION: During the war did any power at war with Germany give you funds?
ANSWER: No.
QUESTION: Do you know what the three letters OSS mean?
ANSWER: Yes.
QUESTION: What do they stand for?

ANSWER: They stand for an American organization.

QUESTION: And you were not connected with that organization?

ANSWER: I was in contact on a friendly and political basis with the members of that organization.

Gisevius had answered truthfully. He always conducted himself as the independent representative of a movement to free Germany of Hitler. Neither he nor his associates served as the agents of a foreign power or asked or received any promise of future consideration for service in what was viewed as a common cause.

There was a good deal of sparring on both sides before I met Gisevius. He was a vice-consul in the German Consulate General in Zurich; I was an official of the American Government and attached to the Legation in Bern. Our countries were at war. A meeting between us was hardly according to the protocol. I had learned all I could as to the character of the man I was to meet and I assumed he did likewise. He was well known to church leaders in Geneva in whom I had full confidence, had been a friend of Niemöller, and was introduced to me by my close associate and chief adviser on German matters, Gero von S. Gaevernitz, an excellent judge of German character. Gaevernitz, an American whose German father had been a leading liberal professor in the universities of Freiburg and Breslau, had a number of close personal friends among prominent anti-Nazi Germans and knew who could be trusted. His friends in turn realized that he would be careful not to jeopardize their security, knowing that their lives and their families' lives were at all times at stake. From this mutual trust sprang the kind of relationship which enabled us to work closely with the anti-Nazis in Germany.

Gisevius, of course, had every reason to be cautious. An indiscretion would not only have been fatal to him, as he was then traveling back and forth between Zurich and Berlin, but might have endangered the conspirators in Germany. Nor was he the type of man who could easily pass unnoticed. Six feet four inches in height and built to proportion—in our underground parlance we called him "Tiny"— so near-sighted that he was not called for army duty, he looked more like a learned professor of Latin or Greek than a member of that most dangerous profession in the world, a conspirator in the German underground. His activities were cloaked under the disguise of membership in Admiral Canaris's service and assignment to the German Consulate General in Zurich. Despite long association with secret and illegal activities, he never seemed able to master his explosive desire to say what he thought about the Nazis. Fortunately, people interpreted his outspoken views as merely a "come-on" to lure people into indiscretions, a favorite technique of the Nazis.

Gisevius was a member of the conspiratorial group within the Abwehr. A close friend of Admiral Canaris and General Oster, he had been sent to Switzerland by them to develop contacts with the outside world which would aid the plot against Hitler. Quite naturally they hoped that they could arouse some interest on the part of the Western Allies, particularly the United States and England.

In the course of my work in Switzerland I met a few other Germans who had the same general outlook as Gisevius. These men felt that a victory of Nazism and the extinction of liberty in Europe and possibly in the world, was a far greater disaster than the defeat of Germany. In fact, they felt that Germany's rebirth could he achieved only through the defeat of Hitler, and they wanted to accomplish that defeat as rapidly as possible and before the kernel of civilization in Germany was destroyed by total war. They wanted the Allies to win before Germany was ground to bits and all values, material as well as moral, disappeared. They believed that there was something remaining on which to build a new Germany. They looked primarily to the West for this, but often with a veiled threat that if we refused to hold out any hope to them they would have no choice but to throw themselves into the arms of Russia.

It was only gradually, as mutual confidence was established, that I began to get the first details of the organization and plans of the German resistance movement.

My contacts with Gisevius had to be protected with every precaution we could devise. We would generally meet late at night, either in Zurich or in Bern, under the protective covering of the Swiss blackout, which made it almost impossible to identify or to follow anyone. But one danger was ever present, namely, that our codes would be broken. I remember well the day in February of 1943, during one of my early meetings with Gisevius, when he told Gaevernitz and me that he feared we would have to stop seeing each other. He took his little black notebook out of his pocket and pieced together the general contents of a considerable number of telegrams which had been sent from Bern to Washington. He had just returned from Berlin and by chance his friends in the Abwehr had learned that the German deciphering services had succeeded in breaking one of the American codes. Fortunately, it was not my own code and I had not used it for sending any operational messages, but as I was then short of code clerks I occasionally had fallen back on this particular code to send general political reports. One of the deciphered messages was a report on the Italian situation and contained what proved to be a fairly accurate picture of the dissension in the Italian ranks and of the anti-German group which, even early in 1943, formed around Badoglio, Grandi, Ciano and others. According to Gisevius this deciphered telegram had been laid on Hitler's desk and sent by him to Mussolini with his compliments. A few days later Ciano disappeared from his post as Foreign Minister and went to the Vatican. I was never able to discover whether this was coincidence or whether this cable was the cause.

In any event, from that time on this code was used only for messages which we were quite willing or even anxious to have the Germans read, and over the months we discarded it entirely. To have stopped using it immediately would have told the Germans that we knew they had broken it. From then on, as far as we could ever find out, and now the Gestapo records are for the most part open to us, the Germans never succeeded in deciphering any of the messages I sent, and I had the satisfaction of knowing that no one who worked with me was ever jeopardized through deciphered telegrams. It was worrisome business, however, and I never put a cipher message on the air which gave specific facts about the underground without a feeling of apprehension. Of course, we continually changed the code names of all those who were working with us in places of danger.

The incident of the broken code actually brought Gisevius and me closer together. For me, it was strong evidence of his sincerity. He became convinced that I used every precaution in handling his reports, and I began to get acquainted with the secrets of the German underground.

At about the time I first met Gisevius I was also put in touch with Adam von Trott zu Solz, of the German Foreign Office, a leading figure in the Kreisau Circle. For reasons of security I never met him personally. He made only two trips to Switzerland during the latter years of the war, and had to be extremely cautious. But on both occasions I was able to get a statement of his views.

During his visit in January, 1943, he reported that his fellow conspirators in Germany were deeply disappointed because the Western powers had given them no encouragement. Here is what he had to say:

The answer is always given [to the anti-Nazis] that Germany

must suffer military defeat. Hence they conclude it is useless to continue the conversations in view of the failure of the Western powers to understand that the Germans are themselves an oppressed people who live in an occupied country and that tremendous risks are taken by the opposition in continuing its activity. As a result, the opposition believes the Anglo-Saxon countries are filled with bourgeois prejudice and pharisaic theorizing. There is a strong temptation to turn East. The reason for the eastward orientation is the belief in the possibility of fraternization between the Russian and German peoples, although not between the present governments. Both have broken with bourgeois ideology, both have suffered deeply, both desire a radical solution of social problems which transcends national limits, both are in the process of returning to the spiritual (but not the ecclesiastical) traditions of Christianity. The German soldier has respect, not hatred, for the Russian. The opposition believes that the decisive development in Europe will take place in the social, not in the military, realm. When the campaign in Russia stalls, after the German army has been thrown back, a revolutionary situation may arise on both sides. Fraternization between Germans and imported foreign workers is also an important element. Hitler has been forced to play up to the laboring classes and has given them an increasingly strong position; the bourgeoisie and intellectuals and generals are of less and less importance. Hitler will fall and the brotherhood of the oppressed is the basis upon which a completely new Europe will be built.

A few days later at Casablanca official Allied policy towards Germany was frozen into the formula "unconditional surrender." * Goebbels quickly twisted it into the formula "total slavery," and very largely succeeded in mak-

* Kessel, writing in his diary in 1945, said some of the conspirators were convinced the unconditional surrender formula "jeopardized and possibly destroyed" six years of work by the anti-Nazi opposition. While granting the exaggeration in this, our slogan made it most difficult to drive a wedge between Hitler and the German people. Here is Kessel's argument: "If Churchill or Roosevelt had declared their intentions to annex Greater Germany, that at least would have been a concrete program that could be understood. But what did 'unconditional surrender' mean? A fort can surrender

ing the German people believe that was what unconditional surrender meant.

To stop short of total military victory, to allow Germany any doubt of its total defeat, would have been unthinkable on our part. On the other hand, the Goebbelses and Bormanns were able to use "unconditional surrender" to prolong a totally hopeless war for many months. We were tongue-tied by the fear that any explanation of what unconditional surrender meant might be construed by the Germans as a promise some future Hitler could say had been broken. The Russians were not so affected and made good use of the Free Germany Committee they set up in Moscow to weaken German morale.

Gisevius often took the same general line as Trott, but he was also realistic enough to accept my word for it that there could be no question of Germany surrendering to the West alone. Once convinced, he used his influence with his friends in Berlin to persuade them that it was "one" war and that there would be "one" peace—with the West *and* East.

Throughout the months that followed our first meeting Gisevius was of inestimable help in keeping me informed of the progress of the plot. Also, through him, we were able to help protect some of the conspirators from Himmler. At one stage Himmler was particularly suspicious of General Halder, even though he had been retired as chief of the General Staff. The Gestapo was not satisfied and wanted him eliminated entirely. To accomplish this Himmler sent to Switzer-

and its defendants are taken prisoner until the end of the war. Was this, then, to be the fate of the whole German people—to be prisoners for a limited period of time, or possibly to be permanently enslaved? And if enslaved, who was to be their master? A slave can serve only one master. Were they to be the slaves of the British, the Americans, or the Russians? If unconditional surrender did not mean slavery why weren't the German people enlightened? Because if the Allies proclaimed their intentions toward the Germans they would be abandoning the idea of 'unconditional surrender.' Thus Churchill and Roosevelt were caught in the confusion of their own formula. And to this day, three years after it was devised, none of the above questions have been answered."

land agents who purported to come from General Halder to the former German Chancellor Wirth, the convinced anti-Nazi mentioned above. Himmler hoped to trap Wirth into sending incriminating messages to Halder. Gisevius was tipped off, Wirth was warned in time, and Himmler's agents went back empty-handed. Another instance of the same sort occurred when Gisevius rescued from the German Consulate in Zurich some letters incriminating a German industrialist who was secretly fighting the Nazis. Before the report reached the Gestapo in Berlin the German industrialist was warned and escaped to Switzerland a few hours before the order for his arrest was issued.

Gisevius himself had some close shaves. When Himmler was on the trail of General Oster, he became suspicious of Gisevius, and during one of Gisevius' trips to Germany he was interrogated about his contacts in Switzerland. Admiral Canaris, not yet under serious suspicion, stepped into the breach and said he had authorized and approved these contacts. Gisevius was able to return to his Zurich post, but he could not risk further trips to Germany. Fortunately, General Oster arranged that Gisevius' place as liaison between Switzerland and Germany should be taken over by Edward Waetjen, a Berlin lawyer whose mother was an American. Waetjen also was attached to the German Consulate in Zurich, and for some months traveled back and forth. Then he, too, became suspect, and his place was taken by Theodor Strünck, who eventually paid with his life after July 20. Through these three men and others we maintained a constant link with the anti-Nazis in Germany.

In January, 1944, I sent a summary of my conclusions about the conspiracy (called "Breakers" in my messages) to Washington. I reported that it consisted of three tendencies —military, revolutionary and evolutionary. The proponents of the first two believed that Hitler should be disposed of and a new government formed before the end of hostilities.

The proponents of the evolutionary tendency were Eastern-oriented and believed Hitler and his gang should, before history and the German people, drink the dregs of defeat. I added that the majority of "Breakers" favored a Western orientation with sweeping social changes and were apprehensive that developments would drive Germany into the arms of the East.

In February I reported, in one of our most secret codes, the names of the leaders of "Breakers": the Socialist Leuschner, Canaris' right-hand man General Oster, and Goerdeler, the former mayor of Leipzig. Later that month I reported that the defection to the Allies of two Abwehr agents in Turkey had so compromised the whole Canaris organization that Himmler and the SD (*Sicherheitsdienst*) were able to get control of it at last. I feared this development would sever our line of communication with the conspirators, but fortunately this did not happen. A few days later I was obliged to report the arrests of Helmuth von Moltke, Otto Kiep (former Consul General in New York), Frau Hanna Solf, and others.

Early in April, on the basis of messages from Goerdeler and General Beck transmitted by Gisevius and Waetjen, I was able to provide Washington with this summary of the conspirators' position:

The German situation is rapidly approaching a climax. The end of the war in Europe is definitely in sight. In this crisis the resistance group in Germany, headed by Goerdeler and General Beck, state that they are now willing and ready to endeavor to initiate action for the removal of Hitler and the overthrow of the Nazis. This group is the only one in Germany which commands sufficient authority in the army and among certain active military leaders to make the overthrow possible. It is also the only one which has personal access to the Nazi leaders, including Hitler, and sufficient arms available to carry through the action.

The group is prepared to proceed only if they can get some

assurances from the Western powers that upon the removal of the Nazis they can enter into direct negotiations with the Anglo-Saxons with regard to the practical steps to be taken. The group is particularly interested that negotiations be conducted through Washington and London and that they would not have to deal directly with Moscow. The group has in mind a procedure somewhat similar to the one applied in the case of the recent Finnish peace negotiations, only in a reversed sense. The Finns, although at war with both Russia and Great Britain, negotiated with Russia only. Although the group fully realizes that in the case of Germany circumstances are widely different, it bases the above request on the fact that the men who plan the proposed overthrow are of a somewhat conservative makeup, though they would work with any available leftist elements other than Communists. The principal motive for their action is the ardent desire to prevent Central Europe from coming ideologically and factually under the control of Russia. They are convinced that in such event Christian culture and democracy and all that goes with it would disappear in Europe and that the present dictatorship of the Nazis would be exchanged for a new dictatorship. The group points out most emphatically that the dangers of such development should by no means be underrated, especially in view of the completely proletarianized millions now populating Central Europe. The group also says that if the surrender is to be negotiated primarily with Moscow a different set of men, not "Breakers," would do the negotiating. After the overthrow of the Nazis, the German generals now in command on the western front, especially Falkenhausen and Rundstedt, would be prepared to give up resistance and to facilitate the landing of Allied troops. Likewise, arrangements could be made for receiving Allied parachute troops in key points of Germany.

Goerdeler and Beck had also added that time was fast running out, and that while they could give no guarantees of success, they were willing to make the effort. Were we interested?

By that time I was aware that divergent social and political views divided the conspirators. Those with whom we were chiefly in contact reflected the opinions of the Right. Fortunately our information was not wholly one-sided and Gisevius, thoroughly disillusioned by the Prussian military caste, constantly warned us against assuming that "Breakers" was merely a military junta. He told us that the Socialist Leuschner was becoming more and more important in the conspiracy. Trott, who again visited Switzerland in April, secretly met Gaevernitz, who prepared for me the following report of Trott's views:

There exists in Germany a Communist central committee which directs and coordinates Communist activities in Germany. This committee has contacts with the Free Germany Committee in Moscow and receives support from the Russian government. Its power is greatly enhanced by the presence of millions of Russian prisoners of war and laborers in Germany, many of whom have been secretly organized and have come under the direction of Moscow. Their activities are helped by the shortage of German guards.

Constructive ideas and plans for the rebuilding of postwar Germany constantly come from Russia. These ideas and plans are disseminated by the Communists among the German masses chiefly by means of well organized whispering campaigns.

Compared to the above, the democratic countries offer nothing concerning the future of Central Europe. Socialist leaders in Germany emphasize the importance of filling this vacuum as quickly as possible if the ever increasing Communist influence is to be counteracted. The drift to the extreme left has assumed stupendous proportions and steadily gains momentum. If it is permitted to continue, German labor leaders fear that in spite of military victory the democracies may lose the peace and the present dictatorship in Central Europe be exchanged for a new one.

To win the German working class for a moderate and orderly policy of reconstruction the following suggestions are being advanced by the German labor leaders:

1. A series of encouraging statements by the democracies addressed to German labor. These statements should emphasize that the participation of Socialist leaders in any future German government and the collaboration of German labor in the rebuilding of Germany will be welcomed.

2. A statement to the effect that German labor will be permitted and encouraged to organize the German labor movement according to its own wishes without interference from capitalist groups of the West with anti-labor tendencies.

3. A fundamental statement on the future self-government in Germany that includes some indication of how much independence the democracies intend to allow to a German administration. It is recommended that special emphasis be placed on the questions of regional and local self-government.

4. A pronouncement to the effect that the democracies do not intend to follow Hitler's methods and create a puppet government in Germany composed of German quislings to represent Allied interests and to rule over the German people.

5. A message of encouragement from the American government to be passed on confidentially to the Socialist leaders in Germany.

6. Though dropping leaflets over Germany had little effect in the heyday of German victories, German mentality is now susceptible to leaflet propaganda. To be effective, leaflet raids should be separated from bombing raids. Leaflets should be dropped in such large quantities that the Gestapo cannot quickly remove them. Leaflets should be edited in cooperation with the German resistance movement so that they are in harmony with the steadily changing psychological trends in Germany.

7. The close contact between the German Communists and Russia should be balanced by an equally active contact between the German Socialist labor movement and the progressive forces of the West. An active exchange of ideas should be inaugurated.

8. The bombings of large populated areas are rapidly completing the proletarization of Central Europe. Labor leaders therefore suggest that bombings be concentrated as much as possible on military and industrial targets.

Early in May, 1944, Gisevius received from Berlin a plan proposed by the military group in the conspiracy that was still predicated on the idea that the Germans could surrender to the West alone. The essence of the plan was that the anti-Nazi generals would open the way for American and British troops to occupy Germany while the Russians were held on the eastern front. Four tactical operations were suggested. First, three airborne Allied divisions were to descend upon the Berlin area where local German commanders would give them all the cooperation they could. Second, large-scale landings were to be made simultaneously on the German coast near Bremen and Hamburg. Third, reliably anti-Nazi German troops in the Munich area would isolate Hitler and the top Nazis in Obersalzberg. And fourth, a landing was to be made on the French coast. For this last, little cooperation was promised because of the attitude of Marshal Rommel (he did not join the conspiracy until the very last minute, after he saw that our invasion was a success).

Gisevius, who had a low opinion of the generals' political courage, told me that he had already sent word back to Germany that it was useless to hope that we would break faith with our Russian ally. I assured him he was entirely correct. Gisevius got back word from "Breakers" that he should take no further action.

Several weeks passed without any important word from our "Breakers" courier. We learned later that the conspirators in Germany began to realize it would have to be unconditional and simultaneous surrender to East and West. This realization, I believe, helped to bring together the Left and the Right, the military and the civilians, those oriented toward the East and those who wanted to deal only with the West. In any event, the advance of the Allied armies forced the conspirators to bury their ideological differences.

Early in July our trusted messenger, Strünck, came to Switzerland and revealed to Gisevius and Waetjen the details of the plot to assassinate Hitler. On July 12 I informed Washington that "dramatic developments may be impending up north. Hope for full report tonight. Ruthless repression, is, of course, a possibility, even a probability." I added that Gisevius was leaving immediately for Berlin to participate, that Goerdeler was compromised and had been forced into hiding, and that the Berlin chief of police, Helldorff, and Colonel General Fritz Fromm, Commander in Chief of the Replacement Army and the immediate superior of General Olbricht, had joined the conspiracy.

In a follow-up on July 13 I reported that the conspirators realized they had only a few weeks more to prove that Germans themselves could rid Germany of Hitler and his gang and establish a decent regime and that the threat to German territory in the East and their desire to save as much of Germany as possible from Soviet occupation had given new impetus to their movement. Hence there would probably be an orderly withdrawal in the West, if the plot succeeded, while Germany's best divisions would be sent to defend the eastern frontier. Later I learned that just before Count von Stauffenberg placed the bomb the conspirators agreed to surrender unconditionally to the Russians as well as to the American and British forces as soon as Hitler had been killed.

This is the story, uncolored by afterknowledge, of what we learned in Switzerland of the plot which we called "Breakers" and to which the conspirators themselves gave the code name "Walküre." It proves that before the plot came to a head a serious effort was made to get in touch with the Allies, that the plotters received no encouragement from the West, and that they were told clearly and repeatedly that we had made common cause with Russia in the determination to continue together to a complete and united victory.

In reviewing my notes of those days (July, 1944) I find that the "Breakers" group was encouraged to proceed by a most innocuous statement in the House of Commons by Mr. Attlee, to the general effect that before there could be any fresh consideration of the German situation the Germans themselves should take the first steps to rid themselves of their criminal government. They were also heartened by a statement made about the same time by Prime Minister Churchill, recommending that the German people should overthrow the Nazi government. I urged that some similar statement be made from America as I was convinced that whatever the result of "Breakers" might be, the fact that an attempt was made to overthrow Hitler, whether or not successfully, would help to shorten the war. Nothing of this nature was done.

When Gisevius left Switzerland about a week before July 20 I was afraid it might be the last time I would see him. The Gestapo were on his trail; his trip to Berlin was fraught with every possible danger. But his charmed existence throughout years of plotting was not over. He arrived in time to live through the last hectic days just before the plot was sprung, and after its failure hid in Berlin—one of the very few to escape the Gestapo's round-up of the conspirators. To help shield him we circulated the rumor that he had managed to get back to Switzerland and was hiding there. The Gestapo combed Switzerland up and down.

Gisevius succeeded in sending us the address of his hiding place. After several months of careful planning, and through devious means, we finally got to him a set of excellent Gestapo papers bearing his own photograph but of course a false name. We also sent him one of the secret Gestapo identification disks. With these he traveled safely "On Special Mission" to and across the Swiss frontier. When in January, 1945, he turned up safe and sound in Bern I felt that we had rather turned the tables on the vaunted Gestapo. As a matter of fact Himmler's secret police and intelligence service, while they excelled in recklessness and cruelty, were neither very skilled nor really subtle. Far too many venal, ignorant and crude men were in it for real efficiency.

The German underground tried at several neutral points, in addition to Switzerland, to get in touch with the outside world. Turkey, Spain and even the Vatican had been used, but after Switzerland Sweden was the place where they particularly concentrated their efforts. I have mentioned that in May, 1942, the Bishop of Chichester met secretly in Stockholm with two German churchmen, Dr. Hans Schoenfeld and Pastor Dietrich Bonhoeffer, who were in the anti-Hitler plot. They gave the Bishop a detailed account of the plans to eliminate Hitler, end the war and establish a new government in Germany. A federated Europe was their eventual aim. The Nazi regime was to be eliminated in two stages, first a revolt inside the party, in which Himmler and the SS would be encouraged to destroy Hitler, and then the army would move against the SS and depose Himmler. The Bishop of Chichester carried the news to Anthony Eden. But the British Government was not impressed.

The German underground's most valuable contact in Stockholm was with the Wallenberg family, the well known Swedish bankers. Marcus Wallenberg, Sr., head of the family, had had close relations with Brüning while he was Chancellor, and also with Goerdeler. After the death of Marcus Wallenberg these friendships were continued, particularly by his son, Jakob Wallenberg, who was a member of the Swedish government's commission on economic relations between Sweden and Germany. To Jakob Wallenberg, Goerdeler disclosed his views about the situation in Germany and finally his plans for the Nazis' overthrow. Jakob Wallenberg summarized for me his conversations with Goerdeler:

Very early, probably in 1940, we discussed the possibilities of a coup d'état in Germany. I often stressed the surprise abroad that there was no organized anti-Nazi movement in Germany, especially as it was known that large sections of the German population and many leading personalities were opposed to Nazism. Goerdeler replied that this criticism was partly unfounded as close to 200,000 Germans were or had been in prison or concentration camps because they had opposed the regime. No coup d'état was possible without the aid of the military, and military help was difficult to secure as long as military successes continued.

In November, 1941, Goerdeler informed me of the German defeat outside Moscow. During a visit in February, 1942, he told me that Hitler had discharged and court-martialed a number of officers because of this crucial defeat, although everyone knew Hitler himself was responsible. Most of the officers were exonerated by the court-martial, but after this a bitter feeling against Hitler developed within high officers' circles. Goerdeler was more hopeful about the possibilities.

In April, 1942, Goerdeler again came to Stockholm and suggested that we [the Wallenbergs] should get in touch with Churchill, whom Goerdeler said he had contacted personally before the outbreak of the war. He wanted to have in advance the Allies' consent to peace in case he and his fellow conspirators succeeded in making Hitler a prisoner and overthrowing the Nazi regime. This was not the first time Goerdeler had broached this subject. I always tried to make it clear to him that no advance promises would be forthcoming and, in order to convince him, I arranged a meeting between him and my brother, Marc Wallenberg, who had intimate contact with the British. My brother also categorically declared to Goerdeler that advance promises could not be obtained.

During my later visits to Berlin Goerdeler reverted to this point, and in November, 1942, we had several long discussions. I impressed on him the risks to which he and his associates would expose themselves, as such a matter would be handled by so many in England and the United States that there would always be the danger of a leak. This did not frighten him. I then tried to make it clear that he and his friends should try to bring about such a change irrespective of the attitude of London or Washington. I believe this argument had more effect on him than the risks involved in trying to get Allied encouragement.

He said he would discuss it with his friends and let me know. A few days later he told me that they were convinced that it was right to act without promises from the Allies. On the other hand, he requested that I be available to get in touch with the Allies as soon as the Hitler regime had been overthrown. This I promised to do.

I next met Goerdeler in February, 1943. He said the decision of the Casablanca Conference for unconditional surrender made his work with the German militarists more difficult since some of the military insisted that if the German forces had to capitulate, they wanted Hitler to bear the responsibility for it. On the other hand, the catastrophe at Stalingrad had occurred and this had made some of the military realize something would have to be done to remove Hitler. Goerdeler told me they had plans for a coup in March of 1943 but that he was not sure that it could be carried through because Hitler was taking all precautions and was surrounded by a bodyguard of 3,000 people and hardly dared to appear at the front any more.

In May, 1943, Goerdeler again came to Stockholm. He knew that my brother was in London and asked that he should immediately get in touch with Churchill. I asked him to draw up a memorandum regarding all the points which the new regime would accept, such as punishment of war criminals, war damages, disarmament, democratic regime, etc. Goerdeler gave me such a detailed memorandum. He also requested that as soon as the coup occurred the Allies discontinue bombing German cities in order to show the German people they were well disposed toward the new regime. Furthermore, he desired that as far as possible Berlin and Leipzig be spared during the next few days as the central organizations of the anti-Nazi movement were located at those points and a disruption of communications would make a coup more difficult. I got in touch with my brother, who passed the information on to the British.

In August I received word that Goerdeler wanted me to go to Berlin. I arranged a reason for such a trip and had several conferences with him. His main points were that all preparations were now ready for a coup in September and that the intention was to send a certain Fabian von Schlabrendorff immediately to

Stockholm. He asked me to persuade the British to send a suitable contact man to meet Schlabrendorff. I replied that I should be glad to do this as soon as the coup occurred and that I would inform the Allies that a German, representing the new leaders, was in Stockholm not to negotiate but merely to obtain Allied advice as to how the new government should go about obtaining peace. On these conditions I accepted the assignment.

On this occasion, as many times before, Goerdeler mentioned certain personnel questions. He was especially interested in knowing about Schacht's position. Schacht apparently wished to play a leading role and considered himself suitable for Foreign Minister, not realizing that he had no standing with the Allies and that people were critically disposed toward him. Goerdeler told me that Social Democratic circles in Germany were against including Schacht in the new government, but that he might be made head of the Reichsbank. Goerdeler had already informed me that the intention was, if the coup succeeded, to make General Beck head of the state and that an interim government would be formed with some military men, civil servants and representatives of labor unions and local interests. As soon as possible elections would be held, and Goerdeler thought it likely that the Social Democrats would take the lead. Goerdeler never told me what his own position would be in the new government.

On this and on previous occasions Goerdeler said that advances had been made to them on behalf of Himmler. No reliance was placed on these advances, and it was their intention to take him into custody at the same time as Hitler.

I was awaiting the month of September with great suspense. It passed without anything happening. I had no opportunity of contacting Goerdeler before the end of November, 1943, when I again visited Berlin. Goerdeler declared that two assassination attempts had been made. He said the plans were in no way dropped but that they had been changed in one particular. The original intention was to take both Hitler and Himmler into custody and put them before a "summary" court. But it had become clear that it would be necessary to assassinate them.

This was the last time I visited Berlin and the last time I met Goerdeler. During the winter, spring and summer of 1944 I

145

received several communications from him to the effect that the plans were still alive, that the assassination would certainly take place, and requesting me to abide by the previous agreement. At the beginning of July I received a telegram that State Secretary Planck wished to visit me in Stockholm about July 20, to which I replied that I was away on vacation and would only return the beginning of August. I then received a further message that it was of importance that he have an opportunity to meet me. I agreed to meet him on the morning of July 22. On July 20 the coup took place. Planck, who for some reason had taken over the place of Schlabrendorff, never came. He was arrested and executed. Goerdeler was arrested when he was about to flee to Sweden, subjected to questioning and torture, and executed. Many people, it is said, were arrested on account of memoranda and notes found in his belongings.

I was warned from several quarters not to go to Germany, as my intimate cooperation with Goerdeler was known. In the month of November I received an invitation to visit Himmler, which I did not accept. I do not believe that anything would have happened to me, but I do not consider it entirely unlikely that Himmler might have asked me to perform for his account the assignment which I had accepted for Goerdeler. The fact that I was, of course, not willing to do anything of the sort reinforced my decision not to go.

In Sweden, as in Switzerland, and indeed as in Spain,* Turkey and the Vatican, the conspirators learned that they could not expect promises from the Allies, that they would have to go ahead, if they chose, not in the hope of securing better peace terms, but solely because the duty to cleanse their own house was an absolute one. It was not conditional upon the help or promises of others.

*The attempts of the German underground to make contact with the Allies in Spain are briefly described in the interesting account which Sir Samuel Hoare (Viscount Templewood) has given of his wartime Ambassadorship in Spain. (See pages 277-78, *Complacent Dictator*, Alfred A. Knopf, 1947.)

11. Himmler

In the very last days of the Third Reich the Gestapo made every effort to destroy or hide records which, it knew, would reveal to the world the depth of the Nazi infamy. They waited too long and destroyed little. In one case freight cars loaded with documents, mostly from the Ministry of Justice, but some from the Foreign Office, were derailed near Berlin by Allied bombing. Papers of fascinating importance were scattered along the railway tracks and over adjacent fields. The Russians picked up most of them, especially those from the Foreign Office. But quite a few were found by friends of mine who brought me a file of particular interest, as it supplied a missing link in the evidence I was compiling on the conspiracy; it gave the story of what the top Nazis learned after July 20 about the plot and how they viewed it. It was marked with the German equivalent of "top secret." And well it might have been, for it revealed that Heinrich Himmler, as early as 1943, had evinced an interest in conspiring against Hitler. The file contained the secret indictment of Dr. Johannes Popitz, the Prussian Minister of Finance I have already described, and Dr. Carl Langbehn, a well known Berlin lawyer who had been a Nazi and had turned into an anti-Nazi conspirator.

Langbehn became personally intimate with Himmler some years before the war by a vagary of chance. Langbehn's young daughter returned from school one day with an invitation from a schoolmate to visit her at her parents' home in Bavaria. But she knew only her friend's first name. Her father suggested that she find out the family name, and next day the daughter reported that the name was Himmler and that the father had "something to do with the SS"! She was permitted to go and the visit was returned. The two fathers met and out of a social visit developed a serious political talk. Himmler gave Langbehn his secret Berlin telephone number and said he would be glad to hear from him as he had little opportunity to know people outside his own organization. The two men met frequently and discussed politics with a freedom that would have sent lesser men to a concentration camp.

Langbehn had had a varied legal clientele. It included Nazis and even Communists. At one stage of the Nazis' attempt to convict the Communists of Göring's Reichstag fire, Langbehn offered to defend the Communist leader Ernst Torgler. He did not go through with it. The story was that the Communists offered him a check drawn on a bank in Holland and payable in Dutch guilders. Langbehn is said to have been offended that the Communists thought he took the the case for money and would not have the courage to stay in Germany after the trial.

Langbehn turned against the Nazis when Professor Fritz Pringsheim, who had taught him law, was sent to a concentration camp because he was non-Aryan. Langbehn went to Himmler and secured Pringsheim's release and permission for him to leave the country. That was in 1938.

I first had the story of Langbehn's encounters with the Gestapo from Marie-Louise Sarre, daughter of a well known German art historian and museum director and herself a sculptress. "Puppi," as she was called, outraged by Nazi cruelty had long shown great courage in protecting people from the Nazis. She worked for the conspiracy, to use her own modest phrase, as "an inconspicuous messenger." She was imprisoned for many months, in the cell in the Prinz Albrecht Strasse jail which separated Helmuth von Moltke and General Halder, and narrowly escaped execution for her part in the phase of the conspiracy which implicated Langbehn. She provided me with the following explanation of the efforts of Popitz and Langbehn to bring Himmler into the conspiracy:

The removal of Hitler by the military, plotted for so long, did not make any headway or failed time and again. It is not up to me to give the reasons as I cannot judge them. It is correct, as indicated in the documents, that Popitz, Langbehn and Jessen doubted the ability of the army to make a revolution. They thought they could remove the regime by splitting its strength.

I was present at a conversation with Field Marshal von Bock of the Central Army Group (Russian Front). That was in July, 1943. Bock believed a putsch carried out by Wehrmacht generals only was bound to fail. He consented to participate only on the condition that the putsch would be made *with* Himmler. Only if the SS participated could it succeed. (I remember his words exactly.) Perhaps it is of interest that Bock warned in that conversation about the reliability of General Fromm.

Another reason: The National-Socialist spirit of the Waffen-SS became increasingly doubtful. They felt at one with the fighting Wehrmacht troops, who were unpolitical. Particularly they did not want to have anything to do with the activities of the Gestapo behind the front lines. Langbehn had several talks with an SS general (I have forgotten his name) who gave him a full report on the morale at the front.

The following facts indicate that Himmler might have been favorably inclined toward a military putsch under his leadership:

Himmler's power was greatest during the year 1943. The SS would have obeyed him unconditionally. But within the clique of tyrants he had enemies, of whom Martin Bormann became increasingly powerful and dangerous because he had the unqualified confidence of the Führer.

One might ask, Why was the attempt never made to kill one

of the second or third ranking Nazis? The answer is that Hitler alone was the source of all power. Even Himmler would have become less dangerous the moment Hitler was eliminated. The hollow structure of the party would have collapsed like a house of cards if deprived of its head.

In 1933 when Hitler seized power and distributed the spoils of government among his henchmen, Himmler was merely commander of the small—but tough—special body-guard, the SS—far less powerful than Ernst Röhm, commander of the Storm Troopers, of which the SS was only a sort of elite branch. Himmler received the relatively minor post of chief of the Bavarian police, subordinate to many a party comrade who had joined much later than he. But in a very short time Himmler obtained one position of power after another. In 1943 he had just taken over the Ministry of the Interior. Why should he stop there? Was it not possible that he could be induced to take the next step?

Difficult and highly dangerous as it was to approach him on the subject, Langbehn was willing to risk it. Langbehn had reason to believe that Himmler, too, was discontented and critical of his master's "intuition" and felt he could do things much better than the Führer. Himmler, misled by vanity and intoxicated by the power of his secret police organization, never realized that he had no popular following within Germany and was universally loathed outside. Hence he was psychologically ready to be approached by those in the conspiracy who saw in this maneuver a chance to drive a wedge between Hitler, Bormann and Co., and the SS.

The indictment of Popitz and Langbehn, found along the railroad tracks, which was prepared for the guidance of Judge Freisler, reveals not only the feelers which were put out in the Himmler camp but also the extent of the Gestapo's knowledge of the conspiracy up to that time. The reader should remember, however, that it was written to whitewash Himmler; that the plotters, Popitz and Langbehn, lied wherever necessary to save fellow conspirators not already dead or too deeply implicated to be saved; and that the Nazi prosecutor minimized or tried to ridicule the conspiracy.

The indictment is dated September 25, 1944, and signed by Dr. Lautz, who was prosecuting attorney.

I accuse the defendants of the following acts:

Until 1943-44, as members of a numerically small clique of conspirators, together with defeatist officers, they conspired within the country against the state and endeavored to remove the Führer by an act of force, even by assassination, in order to overthrow the National-Socialist regime, attain state and military power, and end the war by undignified negotiation with the enemy.

As traitors to Germany they have excluded themselves from the community of the German people.

The accused, Popitz, studied law at several universities at home and abroad and passed the examinations qualifying him for a high civil service career. After serving for a number of years in the Prussian administration, in 1913 he became an assistant in the Prussian administrative court. Some time later he was transferred to the Prussian Ministry of the Interior. After the First World War he entered the Reich Ministry of Finance and in 1919 became assistant chief of a division in that ministry. Later Dr. Popitz became a departmental director in the Ministry and finally, from 1925 to 1929, under secretary. He then left the government service and became a professor at the University of Berlin. At the end of 1932 he became Reich Minister without portfolio and at the same time Reich commissar for the Prussian Ministry of Finance.

After the National-Socialist assumption of power Dr. Popitz took over the Prussian Ministry of Finance at the express wish of the Führer and Reichsmarshal Göring and was appointed Prussian minister of state. In this capacity he attended all meetings of the Reich cabinet and was entrusted by the Führer with numerous tasks outside his special field of activity. Dr. Popitz did not belong to any political party before the assumption of power but voted for the former German National People's Party. On January 30, 1937, he was awarded the Golden Party Badge by the Führer and thus became a member of the party. On the basis of the facts stated in the indictment, Dr. Popitz has been ousted from his office as Prussian minister of state and expelled from party membership.

The accused, Dr. Langbehn, is the son of a German planter in the Netherland Indies. After his ninth year he received his education and training while living with relatives in Germany. As his parents lost their fortune during the inflation he worked in a factory from 1922 to 1923, thus interrupting his university studies. In order to obtain a job he joined a Socialist trade union. Later he resumed his study of law and in 1927 passed his final examinations. Shortly thereafter he was admitted to the bar in Berlin and practiced law until his arrest.

After the assumption of power, Dr. Langbehn participated voluntarily in several maneuvers of the new German Army and was commissioned a lieutenant in the reserve corps. When the present war broke out he was called for military duty but was initially used in the Abwehr because of his knowledge of languages. He volunteered later for service at the front but was soon recalled to a position in the military economy. For a time, before the assumption of power, Dr. Langbehn had been a member of the former National People's Party but in 1929 had connections with the N.S.D.A.P. and became a member in 1933. On the basis of the charges in this indictment, Dr. Langbehn has been disbarred and expelled from the N.S.D.A.P.

The defendants met toward the end of 1941 or in the beginning of 1942 and soon became good friends.

The accused Dr. Popitz claims that he initially welcomed the assumption of power by National Socialism and that he made every effort to assist in the construction of the new state. During the years before the outbreak of war he became increasingly critical of various internal political measures of the German government and claims to have become apprehensive lest the road the Führer was following would lead to disaster for Germany. He claims to have come to the conclusion that the foreign policy of the Führer and Foreign Minister von Ribbentrop would endanger the existence of the German Reich.

When the present world war broke out, Dr. Popitz revealed his apprehensions to the former Colonel General Beck, whom he had known for some time. Beck expressed similarly pessimistic views and doubts that it would be possible to bring the war to a successful conclusion. They discussed the attitudes of leading generals, who, in Beck's opinion, considered the situation serious but would not yet consent to take deliberate action against the Führer. Shortly before the campaign in the West began in 1940 Popitz tried to induce Field Marshal von Brauchitsch to intervene with the Führer, but Brauchitsch refused.

In the course of further conversations Beck re-emphasized his pessimistic views. However, he refused to answer Popitz's question as to whether the generals were prepared to act and declared that that was a matter for the Wehrmacht to decide. He hinted that "prominent civilians" were discussing what might be done in respect to both domestic and foreign policy in the event of a change of government.

At this time Dr. Popitz received a visit from Lord Mayor Dr. Goerdeler, whom he had known before. Dr. Goerdeler explained that he had learned from Beck that he, Popitz, was also greatly troubled. Goerdeler asserted that the only possibility of salvation was for the Wehrmacht to seize power and form a new government. He then asked whether Dr. Popitz would participate if the Wehrmacht were to oust the National Socialist regime. Dr. Popitz consented. To his question as to which military leader was being considered to head the new government, Dr. Goerdeler answered that this was in Beck's hands and that he could not mention any names.

In the course of the next few years Dr. Popitz had a number of conversations regarding the preparations for the proposed coup d'état with Beck, Dr. Goerdeler, and their mutual friend, the former Ambassador von Hassell. Former state secretary Planck and former university professor Jessen, who served as captain with the Chief Quartermaster, also participated in subsequent conversations. During these conversations Hassell declared that he thought an acceptable peace from the enemy might still be obtained. Preliminary feelers would only be possible, however, if a government capable of negotiating were established in Germany, since Great Britain would refuse to negotiate with the Führer and Foreign Minister von Ribbentrop.

In the course of these conversations it became clear that the sick and embittered Beck, who was so pessimistic about the military situation that he believed only a miracle could save the Reich, was to become Chief of State and Goerdeler Chancellor of the Reich, while the army leader chosen to lead the military action against the Führer and the regime would become the supreme commander of the Wehrmacht. Dr. Popitz was, at first, of the opinion that after the Führer had been pushed aside Reichsmarshal Göring should be at the top.

The other conspirators, however, rejected this suggestion, just as they rejected the possibility of a monarchy. Preparations were to be made for a bloodless seizure of the state by the Wehrmacht. A state of siege was discussed, as well as a plan by which the commanders of the military districts would be charged with the removal of the present leaders of state and party and the temporary maintenance of order in their zones. Dr. Popitz knew that the military preparations were in the hands of the former General Olbricht, who was assured of the cooperation of the former president of police, Count Helldorff, regarding preparations in Berlin.

Dr. Popitz held conversations with both these men without obtaining any of the technical details of the plans for the proposed coup d'état. Beck intimated that a number of military leaders were going to deliver an ultimatum demanding that the Führer resign. But the conviction grew that this scheme would not be successful, and it was decided that the Führer would have to be "removed somehow." How the removal was to be effected was not discussed in the presence of Dr. Popitz. He was told that the preparations were entirely in the hands of Olbricht and Beck and that the task of the civilians was to prepare the civil measures to be taken after the coup.

During discussions on this point with Beck, Goerdeler and other conspirators, Dr. Popitz became increasingly opposed to

Dr. Goerdeler. While Goerdeler envisaged a system of popular representation, Popitz rejected this as absolutely impossible, and advocated continued authoritarian government. In the course of these discussions on the reconstruction of the Reich Dr. Popitz submitted a written proposal for a centralized state structure. While Dr. Goerdeler wanted to revive a competitive economy, Dr. Popitz advocated a strictly regulated economy for a long time, if not forever. The strongest differences of opinion, however, arose over labor questions. Dr. Popitz knew that Goerdeler had connections with former Social Democratic trade union leader Leuschner and others whose aim was to create a single unified trade union. Dr. Popitz emphatically opposed such an organization of workers and labor's influence in politics, and, in fact, any concessions to labor. Popitz informed Beck of his opposition to these plans of Goerdeler, without converting him to his point of view.

Differences of opinion between Dr. Goerdeler and Dr. Popitz also arose over who should get the important posts in the new government. Popitz opposed Beck's choice of Goerdeler for Chancellor, and suggested a general of his acquaintance instead. He himself refused the Ministry of Finance, which Goerdeler offered him, explaining that he preferred to be Minister of Education.

In the course of these discussions Popitz also came in contact with a clique hostile to the state which had formed around Count von Moltke. Former First Lieutenant Count von der Schulenburg, who belonged to this circle, visited Dr. Popitz on several occasions to inform him that Moltke's group considered Goerdeler reactionary and unpopular and did not want him to be Chancellor.

Because of these differences, Dr. Popitz and Dr. Goerdeler became estranged and their relations finally ceased altogether.

When defendants Dr. Langbehn and Dr. Popitz came to know each other better in the fall of 1942 they discovered, in talking politics, that they more or less agreed in their pessimistic views of the military situation. They felt that peace feelers were in order. Dr. Popitz asked Dr. Langbehn, whose profession took him abroad during the war, whether he thought peace feelers were possible or whether the person of the Führer was an insurmountable obstacle. Dr. Langbehn indicated that in talks with a Swiss friend he had gained the impression that peace negotiations with our Western enemies were not out of the question. He said that on the basis of several talks with this friend and representatives of hostile powers, some of which he had had with the knowledge of German officials, Great Britain and North America might be favorably inclined toward peace with the Reich, for fear of Bolshevism and for other reasons, but had misgivings regarding the erratic genius of the Führer, whom they considered an unreliable treaty partner. Dr. Langbehn added that he thought these doubts of the enemy would disappear if men of whom they approved guaranteed that Germany would observe treaty obligations.

Dr. Popitz replied that for the sake of obtaining peace a change of government was certainly desirable and informed Dr. Langbehn of the existence and status of the treasonable efforts in which he himself had participated. Dr. Popitz had little hope, however, that revolution from above would be successful. He stated that the generals thought their decorations more important than their country and ironically referred to Dr. Goerdeler as a "country pastor" and "a political traveling salesman trying to scrape up an opposition."

During conversations in the winter of 1942-43, in which Hassell, Planck and Jessen also participated, Dr. Langbehn learned more about the conspiracy. By chance he also met Dr. Goerdeler. In conversations with Goerdeler, Popitz and others, Langbehn gained the impression that they had all pinned their hopes on the generals and were now discouraged. This was undoubtedly the case with Dr. Popitz.

Dr. Langbehn made it clear to Dr. Popitz that he too considered the person of the Führer an obstacle for peace with the Western powers and that he considered Foreign Minister von Ribbentrop utterly incapable. But Dr. Langbehn and Dr. Popitz were afraid the overthrow of the entire National Socialist regime would result not only in the end of the war but in internal chaos. This consideration led them to favor that kind of a change in Germany's political and military leadership that would not impair the power and authority of the SS. This meant enlisting the cooperation of the Reichsführer-SS Himmler himself in their treacherous plans. For this purpose the personal and official relations with the Reichsführer-SS of which Dr. Langbehn boasted were to be utilized.

Dr. Langbehn explained that in his opinion the Reichsführer-SS and his entourage also considered the situation very grave, and that he hoped Reichsführer-SS Himmler could be induced to persuade the Führer to resign and thus remove the obstacle to negotiations with the enemy governments. Himmler was to take over the state and to form a government capable of negotiating. Dr. Popitz thought that in the event of the Führer's refusal force should be used, and agreed that Dr. Langbehn should arrange a meeting with the Reichsführer-SS. Popitz was to suggest to the Reichsführer-SS that he induce the Führer to relinquish the military leadership in favor of a special military staff which was to be formed, and to consent to a change of government, especially in the Foreign Ministry. The closest friends of Dr. Popitz, especially Planck and Jessen, were informed. However, they called this plan an illusion. Dr. Goerdeler, who was also informed, did not advise against it, but did not think that the plan would be successful. Beck was not informed.

About May, 1943, Dr. Langbehn began arranging for such a meeting through SS-Obergruppenführer Wolff, whom he knew. The preliminaries were interrupted by a prolonged illness of Wolff and dragged on until the late summer. Dr. Langbehn explained to Wolff that the war could no longer be won by Germany and that from his talks abroad, he had gained the impression that a tolerable peace could still be obtained for the Reich. However, the English did not see a reliable treaty partner in the Führer and desired a small group of intelligent, sober, and reliable persons such as the Reichsführer-SS and Dr. Popitz. He, Dr. Langbehn, therefore wished to arrange a conversation between the Reichsführer-SS and Dr. Popitz. SS-Obergruppenführer Wolff, who consented to the conversation because he wanted to find out where the efforts of Dr. Langbehn and Dr. Popitz would lead, pointed out that the Reichsführer-SS stood loyally with the Führer and could not break faith. Dr. Langbehn replied that above faith in the Führer was duty to the entire German people. Also, Langbehn said, the Führer could be given some sort of "honorable position in retirement" so that he could occupy himself with his muses and artistic interests, but not with politics. Wolff replied that he would inform the Reichsführer-SS and that a reply would be forthcoming.

Early in August, 1943, Dr. Popitz asked Dr. Langbehn to his home to meet a friend from the eastern front, General von Tresckow, who was unknown to Dr. Langbehn. Tresckow expressed doubts that the Wehrmacht officers who belonged to the clique of conspirators would act. To lay siege to the Führer Headquarters would not be possible, he insisted, because under the existing chain of command not the slightest troop movement could be ordered without the Führer's knowledge. When Dr. Langbehn and Dr. Popitz told him that they were arranging a conference with the Reichsführer-SS on how to establish a military leadership independent of the Führer, von Tresckow declared that under such circumstances the old plan of isolating the Führer's Headquarters could be carried out. He therefore praised Popitz's plan and later said to Dr. Langbehn that "he would have to swallow the bitter pill and go into the lion's den."

At a meeting on August 21, 1943, SS-Obergruppenführer Wolff informed Dr. Langbehn that the Reichsführer-SS would receive Dr. Popitz in his office on August 26, 1943. Dr. Langbehn took occasion to say again to SS-Obergruppenführer Wolff that the war could not be won by Germany, that peace feelers were necessary, and that Dr. Popitz held the key to reorganization of state and army. Dr. Langbehn left no doubt that the proposed conversation aimed at reducing the power of the Führer. He asked SS-Obergruppenführer Wolff to encourage the timid and reticent Dr. Popitz by taking the initiative in the forthcoming conversation with Himmler.

This conversation took place on August 26. Dr. Langbehn accompanied Dr. Popitz to the meeting place, the Reich Ministry of the Interior, which had just been taken over by the Reichsführer-SS. During the conversation, which took place without witnesses, Dr. Popitz stated about the following:

Everybody had anxieties nowadays and he was glad of an opportunity to talk them over. His had been serious for some time but were of a general nature. Corruption had increased tremendously and would become unbearable in the long run. The Gauleiters were no exception. Many were looked upon as tyrants, but the real tyrants were actually in higher places. The people were wondering: What does Himmler want, does he want to start a campaign of terror, or does he really want to establish order? If he wants to do the latter quietly and reasonably, the state would again be on firm foundations and the people's faith in the National Socialist ideology would revive. Then firm authority could again be established. Dr. Popitz saw no overwhelming danger in this.

But, of course, it was necessary to discuss internal questions. The administration was in a hopeless tangle. What was the war situation? This was a constant source of anguish. Would the eastern front hold? Was the military leadership what it should be? There was no unity. It was embodied only in the Führer. If that became too accentuated, the Führer principle would prove impracticable. It was impossible to win the war. Dr. Popitz wondered only whether it would be totally lost or whether it could end in a stalemate. But for this a well known personality would be needed, someone with a name, a person of decision and courage. The Führer is a genius, but he follows his own laws. This did not imply criticism. Still the hour required a citizen to have the courage to explore all possibilities and see what could be done.

There were reasons to believe that Great Britain and the United States see a great danger in Bolshevism. For this and other reasons there is a possibility for peace negotiations. Such negotiations are impossible as matters now stand; they would be conceivable were it evident to the enemy that the Führer was surrounded by men with whom negotiations could be undertaken. They would not negotiate with Ribbentrop. The Führer would have to associate himself with personalities really acceptable to the enemy, and not with low and corrupt creatures. These problems are not insoluble, even for the Führer. The war must not be lost. The Führer has the right to know about everything. He, Popitz, was at Himmler's disposal, but would prefer to remain in the background.

During this conversation, which also touched upon other internal political matters, Dr. Popitz also mentioned to the Reichsführer-SS persons who might be considered for leadership of the army and the Foreign Office. The conversation was to be continued shortly.

While Langbehn and Obergruppenführer Wolff had been waiting in an adjoining room Dr. Langbehn confided to Wolff that he hoped Dr. Popitz would speak frankly and not be too careful. Only a frank discussion could make sense, he said, even if "one risked one's head." He went on about how necessary it was that intelligent and farsighted men re-establish a lawful state in Germany and that the almost unbearable arbitrary power would have to disappear.

The following day another conversation between Dr. Langbehn and Wolff took place in which the latter announced that there was to be another talk between the Reichsführer-SS and Dr. Popitz soon. Dr. Langbehn asked if he might be allowed to participate so as to get Dr. Popitz to speak up and mention the question of reducing the Führer's powers and reorganizing the government. Dr. Popitz had told Langbehn that nothing had really come out of his talk as he had not wanted to bring up the critical points himself.

In order to be able to make concrete suggestions to Himmler regarding a new military leadership, Dr. Popitz got in touch with the former Field Marshal von Witzleben through General Olbricht. He asked Witzleben if he could tell Himmler that he, Witzleben, was willing to assume the supreme command in case Himmler joined the plot. Von Witzleben said he would be if the Reichsführer-SS himself approached him with this suggestion. Dr. Popitz promised to bring this to the attention of the Reichsführer-SS.

Dr. Popitz, who did not conceal his conversation with the Reichsführer-SS from the other conspirators, also talked with Count Helldorff and told him there was a possibility that the Reichsführer-SS might assume power if that were the only way to negotiate abroad.

In September Dr. Langbehn was arrested by the Secret State Police [Gestapo]. The second conversation between Dr. Popitz and the Reichsführer-SS did not take place.

During the ensuing months Dr. Popitz remained almost isolated. To his old disagreements with Goerdeler there was now added the resentment of the co-conspirators, primarily Beck, because he had approached the Reichsführer-SS independently and thus endangered their plans. Dr. Popitz learned from Professor Jessen that the clique of conspirators continued to plot, but no longer considered Dr. Popitz one of themselves. Around the beginning of June, 1944, Dr. Popitz asked Beck straight out if there were still a possibility of action on the part of the military and why he was no longer kept informed. Beck answered evasively that certain people, by whom he seemed to mean Dr. Goerdeler and former trade union leaders, did not wish Popitz to participate in the plot since he has been a minister of the Third Reich and was discredited in many eyes. Dr. Popitz demanded to be told if any plans were still being pursued, to which Beck replied that it was not out of the question. Dr. Popitz claims not to have known of the preparations by Count von Stauffenberg for the assassination attempts or the dates planned for them.

The accused Dr. Popitz has fully admitted the facts as stated above.

The accused, Dr. Langbehn admitted the facts stated above insofar as they concerned him but only after indulging in considerable subterfuge and contradictory statements. He claimed he realized Dr. Popitz had plans for high treason but he insisted he did not consent to them and was merely trying to circumvent them by playing Dr. Popitz into the hands of the Reichsführer-SS. Dr. Langbehn stated he never doubted the latter's faith in the Führer. He had believed, he admitted, that the Reichsführer-SS might participate in the legitimate part of Dr. Popitz's desires, to wit, the establishment of a new Wehrmacht staff and the revitalization of German policy under a new Foreign Minister. However, he acknowledged that Dr. Popitz had made use of his, Langbehn's, stupidity. He denied that he believed in the treasonable plans of Beck, Goerdeler and the other conspirators.

These claims of Langbehn are disproved by his own statements. They cannot be believed, because were they true he would have denounced the plans of the conspirators soon after his arrest in September, 1943, in order to clear himself. Furthermore, the statements by Dr. Popitz refute his defense.

Both of the accused recognized that the use of force against the Führer was part of the plans of the clique of conspirators into which they tried to inveigle the Reichsführer-SS. Clearly they expected determined opposition by the Führer which might have resulted in bloodshed and the death of the Führer. This eventuality they accepted.

I petition that the two defendants be brought to trial before the People's Court.

Miss Sarre read this indictment and made some interesting comments. It was not correct, she said, that Planck and Jessen had advised against drawing Himmler into the plot. Presumably Popitz had tried to avoid implicating them, as well as General Beck and General Olbricht, who were in agreement with the plan, at least in the summer of 1943. It was true, she said, that Popitz had opposed Goerdeler on the course to follow after the overthrow of the Nazi regime, as Popitz feared a complete collapse of all authority in the Reich if social and decentralization measures were attempted with the speed contemplated by the conspirators. From other evidence it seems clear that the Beck-Goerdeler group wished to have nothing to do with the approach to Himmler but, in the early days, did not object to anything which ex-Nazis like Popitz and Langbehn could do to create confusion in the Nazi ranks.

Langbehn's arrest, which ended the conversations with Himmler, came about in a curious way. In September, 1943, he went to Switzerland, to sound out his Allied contacts on the idea of using Himmler to unhorse Hitler. A coded message sent by some Allied agency, neither American nor British, was deciphered by the Gestapo. Himmler had many enemies close to the Führer, particularly Bormann, who was jealous of Himmler's increasing influence and power. One of Himmler's own subordinates, the notorious Obergruppenführer Müller, one of the most vicious men in the whole SS hierarchy, was secretly intriguing against Himmler. Himmler's enemies saw to it that the deciphered message reached Hitler. Himmler's hand was forced, he had to take action.

Naturally Himmler had no interest in bringing Langbehn to trial and did not do so until a year later. Popitz, equally implicated, was not even arrested until the general roundup after July 20 when Himmler was able to cover himself by including both men in the general category of conspirators. But even then he saw to it that they should be tried separately and under special precautions. Among the documents in the file of the indictment I found the following letter from Ernst Kaltenbrunner, chief of the security police (SD) to the Minister of Justice:

I understand that the trial of the former minister Popitz and the lawyer Langbehn is to take place shortly before the People's Court.

In view of the facts known to you, namely the conference of the Reichsführer-SS with Popitz, I ask you to see to it that as a practical matter the public be excluded from the trial.

I assume your agreement and I shall dispatch about ten of my collaborators to make up an audience. As to any others present, I request the right to pass on their admittance.

Miss Sarre, who was arrested at the same time as Langbehn, told me that in her numerous interrogations by the Gestapo one question constantly recurred: "When did Dr. Langbehn last see Himmler?" The answer to this question and all evidence of their last meeting was not mentioned in the indictment. In point of fact another meeting had taken place after Langbehn's return from Switzerland, apparently before Himmler learned of the deciphered message. Langbehn told Miss Sarre that he had touched on the elimination of Hitler only in passing, that Himmler had been quite serious, had asked factual questions, but had not tried to find out any names. Miss Sarre also told me that inmates of a neighboring cell in the Prinz Albrecht Strasse jail said Langbehn was tortured only after the death sentence had been pronounced, and even then not to elicit information. Langbehn was one man Himmler wanted to send to his death without talking.

Himmler's flirtation with treason to his Führer was not repeated until, in the very last days, he tried to initiate separate peace negotiations through Sweden. Hitler knew, before the end, that Himmler too had betrayed him. In what is believed to be his political testament he wrote on April 29, 1945: "Before my death I expel the former Reichsführer-SS and Minister of the Interior, Heinrich Himmler, from the party and from all offices of State."

Göring too was expelled and Hitler tells us why: "Göring and Himmler, quite apart from their disloyalty to my person, have done immeasurable harm to the country and the whole nation by secret negotiations with the enemy, which they conducted without my knowledge and against my wishes, and by illegally attempting to seize power in the state for themselves."

12. East or West

The anti-Nazi conspiracy was made up of a heterogeneous group of plotters. They were able to subordinate many of their differences to the common task, but it was their inability to agree whether to look eastward toward Communism or westward toward democracy which was the most serious threat to their unity. A majority of the conspirators favored England and the United States and some even hoped that after they had removed Hitler they might be able to surrender to the West and continue the war against the Soviets. This was known in Washington and London and was one of the reasons they received no encouragement from the United States or Britain. Anything coming out of Germany was naturally viewed with suspicion in the Allied camp, and suggestions of this nature were construed as attempts to break an alliance that was certain to be victorious if it continued to be united.

The East-West problem has plagued Germany for centuries. All too often German politicians have tried to play off the East against the West, or vice versa, siding with one and then with the other, and throwing the European equilibrium out of balance. This oscillation in German policy reflected an old historic division within the German people. The kings of Prussia and the junkers had been beguiled by the autocratic methods of the Czarist governments and later there were those in Germany for whom the totalitarianism of the Kremlin had a similar appeal. The German liberals on the other hand had always favored the democratic West. Bismarck had been able astutely to alternate between the East and the West. But not his successors. And twice in a quarter century Germany found herself fighting both East and West despite her initial determination to avoid a two-front war.

Hitler hated Soviet Russia. But he did not hesitate to make a pact with her in 1939 to make his strange "courtship" of England more effective. Up to the end, Hitler's hope was for conflict between the East and the West. SS General Karl Wolff, who talked with Hitler a few days before the final debacle, told me that Hitler had said to him: "We must hold out a couple of months longer! Then the Anglo-Americans will be fighting the Russians and we will join one side or the other, I don't care which." Hitler did not have his two months; it was only ten days before the Anglo-Saxon and Russian forces met in the heart of Germany, and the conflict he hoped for did not occur.

The conspirators' problem was not one of European power politics. They were realistic enough to appreciate that the Germany which would survive Hitler would not be a military or political power, but under the control of the victors. But which of the victors? Would Germany fare better as a satellite of Communist Russia, which needed her industrial production and technical skill, or as a part of a Western Europe under the aegis of Britain and France? Many reasoned that Russia would be more likely to put Germany to work, to develop it, than Britain and France, Germany's competitors in world markets. But most of the men in the plot had been brought up in the traditions of Western civilization and therefore favored the West. None of the top conspirators was Communist. Of those who turned to the East some were attracted by its dynamic force, but even more were impressed, despite themseles, by the subtle and effective Russian propaganda, while all they heard from the West was a demand for unconditional surrender.

Around Christmas of 1942 Carlo Mierendorff, Theodor Haubach and Emil Henk, Social Democrats of long standing and members of the Kreisau Circle, met at a spa in the Bavarian mountains. Their work against Hitler has already been described. Knowing of the assassination plans they asked themselves: "After Hitler, what?" They saw that Hitler's elimination meant not only the end of the Nazi regime, but a political vacuum. Where would Germany turn? The American and British forces were far away, no early invasion of the Continent could be expected; it was a long road from El Alamein, a victory which had just been won, to the gates of Berlin. So they reached the conclusion that Hitler's disappearance while the Russians were the only power with a great military force on the Continent, might all too easily deliver Germany into the hands of Communism. Germany, surprised by too sudden a peace, would be overwhelmed by Soviet Russia.

According to Emil Henk, these Social Democrats decided to influence their fellow conspirators to postpone Hitler's assassination until the American and British armies had established themselves on the Continent and at least could compete with the East for the domination of Germany. Mierendorff was delegated to persuade Leuschner, and Moltke was chosen to talk the matter over with Beck. Leuschner agreed, though he saw the danger of delay. The shadow of the Gestapo was already over them all and Leuschner had good reason to fear that by the day of invasion the underground would be decimated. Beck's reaction is not known, but since an attempt was made on the life of the Führer early in 1943, it seems likely that he and Goerdeler favored getting rid of Hitler and letting the chips fall where they might.

Every mile of the German retreat in the East increased the

anxiety over Russia's influence and power in the postwar Germany, but it also increased the impatience of the pro-Russian conspirators to get action. The influence of the latter was enhanced by the growing skepticism in Germany over what could be hoped for from the West. Our propaganda consisted of the slogan "unconditional surrender," and was coupled with the bombing of German cities, high civilian casualties and the destruction of thousands of workers' dwellings. That this type of bombing came only from the West made a deep impression on the German masses who ascribed it to a deliberate difference in policy between East and West. They overlooked the fact that Russian aviation was not adapted to that type of bombing—and, moreover, was fully occupied by the strategic necessities of a front stretching some 1,000 miles from the Black Sea to the Gulf of Finland.

As the bombing of Germany had an important political effect upon the German population it deserves more than passing notice. There can be no question whatever that the bombing of German railways and communications and of certain strategic objectives—particularly the synthetic-oil plants and airplane and ball-bearing factories—were of vital military importance. It forced the decentralization of German industry, which greatly reduced efficiency, and then as we destroyed German communications, the scattered factories were unable to get essential raw materials or finished parts.

But the wholesale bombing of cities where civilian objectives were primarily affected, I believe, did little to shorten the war. In World War I a disillusioned but unbombed German population recognized the inevitability of defeat and helped to hasten the surrender. In World War II the bombed-out population turned to the state for shelter, food and transportation away from the devastated areas. If anything, these men and women were more inclined than before to work for and support the state, since they were dependent, homeless and destitute.

I am frank to admit that I was at first mistaken as to the effect of this bombing. The devastating attacks on Hamburg in the summer of 1943, with one of the early uses of phosphorus incendiary bombs on a grand scale, coincided with the sharp decline in German morale which followed the fall of Mussolini in Italy, and had a profound effect. I had the feeling, and so reported at the time, that more of this bombing might bring a collapse in Germany. Some months later I came to the conclusion that I was wrong. German morale not only withstood the bombing of cities, but seemed to stiffen under it. Instead of gaining recruits, the anti-Nazis lost them. One of its important members, Carlo Mierendorff, for example, was killed, and many of their secret meeting places were bombed out and their membership dispersed. Also, the resentment engendered in working class and bourgeois circles weakened the influence of the Western-oriented conspirators and brought to the fore those who thought the only hope was from the Soviets. The anti-Nazi conspiracy, which at its inception had been based on cooperation with the West, became a movement of two more evenly balanced tendencies, one East and one West.

One of the foremost conspirators who desired rapprochement with Russia was Count Werner von der Schulenburg, German Ambassador to Moscow until June 22, 1941. He had tried hard to keep the troubled relations between the two countries in balance—no easy task under Hitler. The Führer said what he pleased about Russia, and Schulenburg had to explain away his remarks at the Kremlin. When he returned home, a disillusioned man, he joined the conspiracy. In the summer of 1943 there was a secret plan that Schulenburg should go to Moscow and arrange a peace with Russia that would lead to a general peace. He intended to obtain the Russian demands about Eastern Europe through personal negotiation with Stalin. The idea of the conspirators was to smuggle Schulenburg through the German lines into Russia. Once on Russian territory, Schulenburg was confident, he could reach the Kremlin. The Central Army Group on the eastern front was selected as the best place for the attempt, and Field Marshal von Kluge is said to have been willing to cooperate. For some reason—the difficulties of getting him through the German lines were alleged—nothing came of it.

At approximately the same time Count von Stauffenberg was acquiring influence among the conspirators. He had gathered around himself several younger army officers and civilians who were attracted by his forceful personality and by his determination to act. Among them was Count Fritz von der Schulenburg, a reformed Nazi and cousin of the Ambassador. Schulenburg's great energy and administrative ability and his position as second in command of the Berlin police had made him an important member of the inner circle of those pressing for early action even before Stauffenberg appeared on the scene. Through his contacts with Trott, Yorck and others of their friends, he had brought the Kreisau Circle closer to the group of military conspirators.

Stauffenberg recognized the over-all leadership of Beck and Goerdeler, but had no sympathy with them politically. He was one of those who were attracted by the resurgence of the East, and believed liberalism to be decadent and the adjective "Western" a synonym for "bourgeois." Gisevius told me Stauffenberg toyed with the idea of trying for a revolution of workers, peasants and soldiers. He hoped the Red Army would support a Communist Germany organized along Russian lines. His views were shared by other conspirators, particularly by certain of the younger men of the Kreisau Circle, including the Haeften brothers and Trott. In the case of some it was a matter of ideology, in other cases it was a question of policy. Some had reached the conclusion that nothing constructive could be worked out with the West. Soviet propaganda had influenced others.

The Free Germany Committee, although only a tool of psychological warfare, impressed many Germans. Germans captured by the Russians on the eastern front were sent back to Germany to spread the Communist gospel. "Free Germany" committees began to form in secret on the eastern front, and to a limited extent in Germany. While British and American planes ruined one German city after another, and London and Washington talked only of unconditional surrender, the Free Germany Committee broadcast on the Moscow radio:

The Soviet Union does not identify the German people with Hitler. . . . Our new Germany will be sovereign and independent and free of control from other nations. . . . Our new Germany will place Hitler and his supporters, his ministers and representatives and helpers before the judgment of the people, but it will not take revenge on the seduced and misguided, if, in the hour of decision, they side with the people. . . . Our aim is: A free Germany. A strong powerful democratic state, which has nothing in common with the incompetence of the Weimar regime. A democracy which will suppress every attempt of a renewed conspiracy against the liberties of the people or the peace of Europe. . . . For people and fatherland. Against Hitler's war. For immediate peace. For the salvation of the German people.

The Russians kept up this propaganda to the end, and when we reached Berlin in May of 1945, the city was already placarded with Soviet propaganda, including these words of Stalin: "Hitlers come and go, but the German people, the German state, remain."

The leading military members of the Free Germany Committee, who were also the leaders of the affiliated Association of German Officers, commonly called the "Seydlitz Committee," were Generals Walther von Seydlitz and Alexander Edler von Daniels. In vain they had tried to bring General von Paulus into the conspiracy at the time of the "Stalingrad putsch." And just before July 20 Adam von Trott is reported to have seen Madame Kollontay, the Russian envoy in Stockholm, in order to establish contact with the Free Germany Committee in Moscow.

The Moscow radio gave a great deal of time and attention to the July 20 conspirators. On July 21 Seydlitz broadcast the following:

The die has been cast. Courageous men rose against Hitler. They have thus given the signal for the salvation of Germany. The power which Himmler holds can be taken from him only by the German people. . . . Generals, officers and soldiers! Cease fire at once and turn your arms against Hitler. Follow only those who will lead you against Hitler. Do not fail these courageous men.

Several days later General Hans von Wartenberg, one of the prisoners taken at Stalingrad, broadcast from Russia:

The leaders of the freedom movement are still alive and in hiding! They count on support from all classes of the German people.

And what came from Washington and London? The attempt on Hitler's life was dismissed as of no consequence. Churchill suggested that it was merely a case of dog-eat-dog. And Judge Freisler, as he passed the death sentence on Count Schwerin von Schwanenfeld, one of the conspirators, taunted him: "Did you hear about the leaflets which the enemy dropped even after your ill-fated plot? In one of them the English say: 'Indeed, those who cooperated, those who engineered it, all of them are not worth anything. At best, they had a perverted love of Germany!' "

Both Washington and London were fully advised beforehand on all the conspirators were attempting to do, but it sometimes seemed that those who determined policy in America and England were making the military task as difficult as possible by uniting all Germans to resist to the bitter end.

Despite the growth of the pro-Eastern wing, Beck, Goerdeler, and the others who were the mainstay of the plot, considered Communism no better than Nazism. But they had to recognize the strength of Stauffenberg's position when he became one of their inner circle.

He was no mere onlooker. He claimed a leading role in policy-making as his right, since he was to organize the actual attempt on Hitler's life. His choice for Chancellor was the Socialist Wilhelm Leuschner. But Leuschner declined, possibly because he did not want to compete with his friend Goerdeler, possibly because he did not want to lead a group friendly to the Soviets. Stauffenberg then suggested Julius Leber, who was well known in army circles and had been the army's liaison with the Social Democratic party. When this and other demands were not met, he threatened to break with the Beck-Goerdeler group and even started to work on his own. Thus, at the very last minute, just before the assassination, the one great essential of mutual confidence and unity was seriously threatened. Only Beck's over-all authority was still respected.

After June, 1944, as soon as it became clear that American and British troops had secured a permanent foothold in France, Stauffenberg's activity redoubled. He proposed that Communists be taken into the coalition. When he was advised against it for security reasons, he induced his Socialist friends to establish contact with the Communist underground, without the consent of the other key conspirators.

On June 22 Leber and Reichwein, representing the conspiracy, and Anton Saefkow, Franz Jacob, and a third man whose name is not known, representing the Central Committee of the Communist underground, met clandestinely. The Communist ZK, or Central Committee, had only recently been reorganized. Saefkow, a onetime metal worker, had been particularly active in the Ruhr region and was a friend of Ernst Thälmann, the head of the Communist party before Hitler came to power. When Saefkow was caught by the Gestapo in Hamburg in 1933, the infamous Terboven, then Gauleiter of the Ruhr region and later of Norway, had him brought to his native Essen where he was so tortured that there was grave doubt of his recovery. It is a miracle how he survived the ten years of concentration camp life which followed. Some time in 1943 he and Jacob succeeded in escaping and in getting to Berlin. Shortly before the Brandenburg leader of the Communist underground had been executed. Saefkow and Jacob immediately assumed leadership.

At the June 22 meeting the proposal was made that the Beck-Goerdeler post-Nazi government would include Communists. Saefkow and Jacob and their unnamed comrade were given the names of some of the leading conspirators. They asked for time to decide, and another meeting was arranged for July 4, at which Stauffenberg was to be present.

The conference never took place. On July 4 the Gestapo arrested Reichwein, and, the next day, Leber, as well as hundreds of leftists who had relations with the Free Germany Committee. It was clear that the Gestapo had penetrated the Communist underground. Saefkow and Jacob were later executed.

A truce between the East and the West within the small ranks of the conspiracy was called. Everyone realized there was time only for one thing, the original purpose of the conspiracy, the removal of Hitler, and little enough time for that.

13. Berlin—July 20, 1944

By July 20 the conspirators were in great jeopardy, and their ranks had been thinned. General Oster was under house arrest. Moltke had been in prison since the beginning of the year. Three days before July 20 a warrant had been issued for the arrest of Goerdeler and he was in hiding. Leber had been arrested.

The actual assassination had been planned for the end of July, but the first abortive attempt was made on the eleventh, not quite a week after Leber's arrest. It has been said the putsch was attempted too early because of Stauffenberg's desire to rescue Leber before he was killed by the Gestapo. In any event, the conspirators knew the Gestapo was closing in. The putsch had become a race with time. Moreover, the conspirators had their families as well as themselves to think of. If the coup failed, women and children would not be spared.

On July 11, Gisevius returned secretly from Switzerland with a last-minute suggestion. He proposed that Goerdeler and he fly to Field Marshal von Kluge, Commander in Chief on the west front, and convince him that for the sake of Germany's salvation he should refuse to obey the Führer's orders and lead his armies against the Nazis back into the Reich. Other commanders, like Rommel and Stülpnagel, would follow suit, and civil war between the army and the Nazis would result. Then the conspirators could act. Beck would have none of it. He wanted no civil strife if it could be avoided.

The wheel of fortune had seemed to turn in favor of the conspirators when Field Marshal von Kluge had been suddenly appointed Commander in Chief in the West, succeeding Rundstedt. They had once approached Rundstedt, who refused, saying he was too old to be a plotter. But with Kluge there was a chance. He had been in and out of the conspiracy before but at the last moment had always had pangs of conscience about his military oath. Now, to the surprise of the conspirators, on his own initiative, he sent a member of his staff, Lieutenant Colonel von Hofacker, to see Beck. The new commander opposing Eisenhower gave it as his opinion that the Normandy front could not hold out longer than two weeks. He said that when he was given the western command he had been deliberately misled by Hitler as to the real strength of the German armies in France. Convinced that the military situation was hopeless for Germany, angered and desperate, he declared to Beck his willingness to support the putsch.

Field Marshal Rommel had similarly committed himself. The glamor general of the once victorious panzer army, the dreaded "Desert Fox," was commanding the principal force (German Army Group B) opposing the Allies in France. He was convinced the Allies would break through into the interior of France at any moment and on July 9, in a stormy meeting with Hitler, he demanded permission to withdraw from Normandy before his armies were cut off. Hitler refused. Immediately after this meeting Rommel got in touch with Hofacker and—conditionally—agreed to work with the conspiracy.

Rommel's "desertion" was only discovered some time later. A few days before July 20 he had been eliminated from any active participation in the events of that day as a result of wounds suffered during an Allied strafing attack. But Hitler took his revenge when he discovered the facts, though Rommel's treason was never admitted to the German people. According to Rommel's son, the Gestapo appeared at Rommel's home in Germany, where he was convalescing. He was given the alternative of committing suicide or facing public trial and certain "inconveniences" to his family. The Field Marshal was offered a vial of poison to help him make up his mind. Rommel said goodbye to his family and entered a waiting automobile. Several hours later a hospital in a near-by town reported his death. He was given a state funeral, but a memorandum was circulated in the highest party circles to the effect that Rommel "did not at all deserve the good name which able propaganda made for him" and that he "could by no means be considered a Nazi." The memorandum, signed by Party Secretary Martin Bormann himself, ended: "Of course, you may not discuss these things."

Unfortunately the Commander in Chief of the Replacement Army, Colonel General Fritz Fromm, had not unequivocally committed himself. Fromm was not an ardent believer in Nazism and, like most of the generals, was disgusted with Keitel's slavish cowardice and his constant intrigues. He had given Keitel a report on the desperate military situation and urged him to do something about it. Keitel had merely shrugged his shoulders and retorted that under the circumstances it was better not to do anything at all. It was assumed that if the plot appeared to be succeeding Fromm would willingly join. After all, he was aware of what was going on in his own office and had once said to one of the conspirators: "And for my sake, don't forget Keitel when you are carrying out your putsch!"

Stauffenberg, whose transfer into Fromm's office, as Chief of Staff of the Replacement Army, was engineered by the conspirators, had cautiously sounded out Fromm, but had found that despite his defeatist attitude he was more concerned about his titles, medals and rank than for the fate of

Germany. It was therefore decided that if Fromm should refuse to sign the conspirators' orders after the assassination, he was to be arrested and replaced by Colonel General Hoeppner.

Hoeppner was one of the first German officers to take tank warfare seriously and commanded Germany's first completely armored army corps. He had helped to win the victories in Poland, France and Russia. But Hitler's "intuition" about strategy in Russia was too much for him. On July 1, 1942, he was court-martialed for advocating a retreat in violation of Hitler's orders. The Nazis wanted to execute him for "cowardice in the face of the enemy," but army pressure saved him. He was only dismissed from the service.

By dawn of the fateful July 20, everything the conspirators could do was done. Upon receipt of word that Hitler was dead, Witzleben would assume command of all German armed forces—land, air and sea. The Replacement Army, under the command of either Fromm or Hoeppner, would restore and maintain order within the Reich. The Berlin Guard Battalion would surround government buildings in Berlin and protect the War Ministry until Replacement Army contingents arrived. General Kortzfleisch, the Nazi commanding general of the all-important Berlin area, Defense District III, would be arrested and replaced by Lieutenant General von Thüngen, a member of the conspiracy. Lieutenant General Paul von Hase, the commander of Berlin itself, was solidly behind the conspirators, as were the majority of his staff.

In addition to the Berlin garrison, the conspirators could count on the reserve troops in the camps at Zossen, Wünsdorf, and the trainees of the army school in Döberitz, all in the immediate vicinity of the capital. Stauffenberg and Olbricht had arranged to station senior officers in these camps who were largely anti-Nazis. Not all of them were initiated into the conspiracy, but it was believed that most of them would support the putsch once it was put in motion. The cooperation of the local police was also expected as the notorious Count Wolf von Helldorff, police president of Berlin, and a convinced Nazi for many years, had thrown in his lot with the conspirators. "We will all have to jump off the Hitler bandwagon some day," he retorted to Judge Freisler at his subsequent trial when the Judge questioned him as to why he had deserted the Führer. Helldorff was to have no part in the new regime but the aid he could give in gaining control of Berlin made him a useful ally.

Here the troops of the Replacement Army were to play the leading role. They were to arrest the chief Nazis, surround SS barracks, arrest the commanders and disarm the men. Simultaneously, each Military District commander throughout Germany would be told by telegram to open the sealed envelope in his safe, which all too prophetically was marked *Walküre,* the name given in German mythology and in Wagnerian opera to warrior maidens who hovered over the field of battle, choosing those to be slain and conducting the worthy to Valhalla.

Like every army in the world, the German army had a standing procedure for operating against internal disturbances. Conspirators on the General Staff of the Replacement Army or connected with the agencies concerned with such plans in the War Ministry, revised this standing procedure in such a way as to set in motion on the day of the putsch the maneuvers that would circumvent the SS and ensure the success of the coup. The new orders were sent sealed and were to be opened by the district commanders only when the code word *Walküre* was sent them from Berlin. The orders provided for the establishment of martial law, suppression of all political activity, occupation of all public buildings by the Wehrmacht. The orders also revealed the location of the Gestapo's secret headquarters, the possible hiding places of top Nazis, and the reliability of army officers in each district. Each order also contained the name of a civilian who was to advise the military commander in his district. The orders were so phrased that if any district commander were to open one in advance (an almost negligible risk in the case of disciplined German officers) the true purport would not be obvious. But after the putsch failed, hundreds were implicated by these orders.

Simultaneously, generals in the field were to arrest Nazi and SS officials under their command. A number of generals, of course, were "in the know" and would act spontaneously. These included Field Marshal Rommel; General Count Heinrich von Stülpnagel, Military Governor of France (not to be confused with his cousin, General Otto von Stülpnagel, also for a time Military Governor of France, but not a member of the conspiracy); General von Falkenhausen, Military Governor of Belgium; and Field Marshal von Kluge.

Once the putsch was under way General Beck was to announce over the official German radio, the *Deutschland Sender,* that Hitler was dead, that he was now Chief of State, that Witzleben was in command of the armed forces, and that there would be a three-day state of emergency in which to liquidate Nazi resistance and form a cabinet. The new cabinet would enter into armistice negotiations immediately.

The conspirators had agreed on a cabinet broadly representative of all anti-Nazi political groups except the Communists. Goerdeler was to be given the Chancellorship, and he had prepared a manifesto that declared the immediate aims of the new regime were terminating war, rejecting totalitarianism and creating a state based on the Christian traditions of Western civilization, with a good bit of state socialism and the nationalization of heavy industry thrown in. Leuschner, the Social Democrat, was to be Vice Chancellor and the likely candidate to succeed Goerdeler if the expected swing to the Left materialized.

Two men were designated for Foreign Minister. If surrender negotiations were first undertaken with the Western powers, Ulrich von Hassell was to get the post. If the new government should have to turn in the first instance to Moscow, then the Foreign Minister was to be Werner von der Schulenburg.

The important Ministry of the Interior, which controls the police, went, not without bitter argument, to Julius Leber, Social Democrat. The Ministry of Culture and Education was assigned to a compromise candidate, Eugen Anton Bolz of the (Catholic) Center Party. It was not finally decided whether the Ministry of War should go to General Friedrich Olbricht or to General Hans Oster. Leuschner won a battle over the Ministry of Information and got it for his fellow Socialist, Theodor Haubach. The Minister of Economics was to be a Catholic, Paul Lejeune-Jung, and the Ministry of Finance was to go to a conservative named Loeser. A Ministry of Reconstruction was to be created, to be headed by Bernhard Letterhaus, a great friend of labor who also enjoyed the confidence of conservative circles, a man whom former Chancellor Brüning described to me as "one of the best."

Many other posts were assigned. Count von Stauffenberg was to be Under Secretary of War. To cement relations between the Socialist and Catholic trade unions Jakob Kaiser would become Leuschner's deputy. And Gisevius, whose Gestapo and Abwehr experience would be useful in routing out the Nazis and preventing a countercoup, was to be Special Adviser on Public Security to the Chief of State.

No date for elections was fixed. Many of the conspirators insisted that general elections could not be held until the country was thoroughly denazified. Until elections the cabinet was to be advised by a kind of senate appointed from

Germany's leading anti-Nazi citizens (the president was to be the Socialist Paul Loebe, former president of the Reichstag) and designees of the heads of the provincial governments. These provincial governorships were also assigned to trusted conspirators.

On July 20 General Beck, and the chief military conspirators and several of their civilian advisors gathered in Olbricht's office in the War Ministry to await the signal from East Prussia. What happened that afternoon in the Ministry, even in its minute details, can be pieced together from the subsequent trials and the reports of the few survivors.

Hoeppner had come in from the country to join them, bringing his uniform in a suitcase (Hitler had forbidden him to wear it after his dismissal). Olbricht was in a confident mood. When he and Hoeppner lunched together, he toasted the putsch and an early peace. They returned to Olbricht's office and waited, with increasing anxiety, for the telephone call from General Fellgiebel announcing the death of Adolf Hitler. No call came.

The suspense became almost unbearable.

At 3 o'clock they learned that an announcement from Hitler's headquarters was expected at any minute.

What did that mean?

Thirty minutes later General Thiele, one of Olbricht's aides, came in to report that he had finally got through to the G.H.Q. at Rastenburg but had only been able to learn that there had been an explosion and that a number of officers were severely wounded.

At this moment, about 3:30, Stauffenberg's adjutant, Werner von Haeften, called from Adlershof airport to report that Stauffenberg and he were safely back in Berlin. He added tersely: "Hitler is dead."

The conspirators sprang into action. Olbricht and his chief of staff, Colonel Merz von Quirnheim, went to General

Fromm's office, told him that the Führer was dead, and asked him to give the general alert to the Replacement Army. Fromm demanded to know how Olbricht knew Hitler was dead. All that Olbricht could say was not enough to convince Fromm. He picked up the phone and, to Olbricht's and Quirnheim's dismay, got Keitel at Supreme Headquarters. Obviously, something had gone wrong. The communication center at Hitler's headquarters was functioning. Keitel told Fromm the Führer was only slightly wounded and demanded to know where Stauffenberg was.

Fromm hung up and turned to Olbricht and Quirnheim. He had made his decision. Hitler was alive and consequently he, Fromm, would take no treasonable action against his oath and his Führer. Olbricht and Quirnheim argued that his duty to his country was greater than his duty to Hitler. Fromm was adamant.

Olbricht then went to get Stauffenberg, who had just arrived from the airport. Stauffenberg passionately pleaded with Fromm. "I saw everything from the outside," he said. "I stood in front of the barrack with Fellgiebel when the explosion occurred. It was as though a fifteen-centimeter shell had hit it. It isn't possible that anyone in there is still alive."

Fromm was unconvinced.

Stauffenberg finally exclaimed: "Field Marshal Keitel is lying as usual. I myself saw Hitler's dead body carried out."

Fromm shrugged his shoulders.

Olbricht then tried another tack. He announced that he and Quirnheim had already issued the *Walküre* orders and that in Berlin and the provinces the Replacement Army was on the march. Fromm flew into a rage. He declared Quirnheim under arrest.

In a desperate last effort to win Fromm, Stauffenberg admitted that he had placed the bomb. "Hitler will destroy our country if we fail to act now," he pleaded.

His frankness increased his chief's fury. Fromm declared

he would arrest everyone present, but the conspirators had foreseen this eventuality. They overpowered Fromm. Olbricht disarmed him and summoned Hoeppner to take over the command of the Replacement Army.*

This appointment was the first act of the "new regime" by the "new" Commander in Chief, Field Marshal von Witzleben.

As Hoeppner entered Fromm's office Fromm was being led away under guard. Hoeppner expressed regret that they should meet under such circumstances and said he had been appointed his successor. Fromm answered:

"I can not help it; I believe you are making a great mistake. I am convinced the Führer is still alive, and therefore I cannot sign your orders."

By then an hour and a half had elapsed since the conspirators had learned of the explosion at Supreme Headquarters.

Olbricht and Hoeppner started to send out the orders to the District Commanders and commanders in the field which were to supplement *Walküre*. Fifty teletypes and eight hundred telephones worked to capacity. Military District commanders and command posts all over occupied Europe were informed of Hitler's death and ordered to occupy strategic key points and specific buildings in their areas. They were given to understand there had been an SS attack upon the Wehrmacht, something the old line soldiers always feared. High SS officers, in some places the entire SS, and party leaders, were ordered arrested. The telegraphers and telephone operators did not question these unusual orders. Germany's only anti-Nazi uprising had begun.

---

* At his trial three weeks later, Hoeppner testified that at this point he already had doubts and that he questioned Olbricht on the legality of this transfer of command. He claimed he demanded a written order. To this his judge, the sardonic Freisler, remarked with not unjustified sarcasm, "Your revolution commenced rather bureaucratically!" He was right. The plotters were trying to stage an "orderly," bloodless revolution against a crowd of gangsters.

At 4 P.M. the commander of the Berlin garrison, Lieutenant General Paul von Hase, began to surround the government quarter with the Berlin Guard Battalion. Peter Yorck von Wartenburg was issuing passes over Stauffenberg's signature to reliable officers. Young von Kleist, Georg von Oppen and Ludwig Hammerstein (son of the General)—all three survived to tell the story of that afternoon—were assigned as aides to Beck and Olbricht. Haeften aided Stauffenberg in getting out the orders. Witzleben motored into Berlin from the headquarters at Zossen and conferred with Beck. He left the Bendlerstrasse obviously dissatisfied. The military support on which the conspirators were counting was not in evidence. The troops which were to take over Berlin were too slow in arriving.

Doubt began to infect the conspirators. Some of them, apparently even Beck, insisted on making sure that Hitler was really dead. They tried, unsuccessfully, to reach Supreme Headquarters.

Several staff officers in the War Ministry, who were not initiated into the conspiracy, became troublesome. To quiet them Stauffenberg called a meeting of all department heads. He explained the situation as he saw it, as he wanted them to see it, and asked them to be loyal to the new regime. One of the officers, a General Specht, flatly said he wouldn't. The chief troublemaker, as expected, was General Kortzfleisch, commander of the Berlin Military District. He was arrested and Lieutenant General von Thüngen took his place.

By this time, between 4 and 5 P.M., some of the alerted troops from the suburbs were reaching the outskirts of the city. Few of their commanders knew what was up.

Around 5 o'clock, Count von Helldorff appeared at the Bendlerstrasse. He accepted the version of events provided by Beck, Hoeppner and Gisevius, who ordered him to put the Berlin police under the authority of the army and await further orders.

At 7 P.M. another report that Hitler was only slightly wounded reached the Bendlerstrasse. The conspirators held an excited conference. They were now irrevocably compromised. District commanders and commanders in the field had received their orders and probably had already taken action. Trusted troops were arriving in the capital. It might still be possible to get the city under control before the Nazis could send reinforcements. The radio station must be seized so Beck could make his announcement, thereby forestalling any statements by the Nazis. This was crucial.

The dilemma of the conspirators revealed the true character of more than one of them. Hoeppner wanted to quit. Beck tried to reassure him. "The report that Hitler is still alive may be a ruse—they know a lot about propaganda," he said.

Hoeppner suggested that Hitler might speak over the radio and ruin everything.

Beck replied: "He has not yet spoken. I shall have to speak first. If he is still alive we shall have to stop him from speaking."

"Isn't that a matter of strength?" Hoeppner asked nervously.

"Let us be strong at this moment—for Germany," Beck answered quietly.

The fact that there were not enough reliable troops in the center of Berlin to seize the radio station at length made the conspirators realize that troops they depended on were not arriving. They also realized that they had made a fatal error in assuming their orders would be obeyed without question because they arrived through regular channels. Too many officers had taken thought before they acted. The plotters had relied on the principle of blind obedience to authority, preached for centuries in the Prussian army. But Nazi doctrines had penetrated the army to a far greater extent than they had thought possible.

General von Knesebeck, the Military Commander of the Vienna district,* called Hoeppner and said he had "conflicts of conscience" because an order from Field Marshal Keitel had arrived and countermanded Hoeppner's orders. He added that the SS who had been arrested had been released. He had no sooner hung up than the assistant commander of the Stettin District called to say Keitel had rescinded Hoeppner's order.

Meanwhile, in Paris the revolt was in full swing. General von Stülpnagel had arrested many of the SS stationed in the French capital. Careful preparations had been made, accordnig to the account of one of the survivors, Friedrich von Teuchert, a member of Stülpnagel's staff. Hofacker and Fritz von der Schulenburg, the latter using his cover as a member of a commission to deal with local disorders, acted as liaison between the conspirators in Berlin and Stülpnagel's group in the Hotel Raphael in Paris. Kluge, Rommel (before he was wounded) and his chief of staff, General Speidel, had also been forewarned that the coup d'etat was to take place. On the evening of July 19, Hofacker, Teuchert, and their co-conspirators held a last secret meeting, and made final preparations to take over control in Paris.

The key figure was Kluge, and, as usual, his courage failed him. As soon as he heard, that July 20th afternoon, that Hitler had survived, he called Stülpnagel to his headquarters, and, despite all that Stülpnagel could say, stubbornly maintained that Hitler's death was a *sine qua non* for his cooperation. "But Field Marshal," Stülpnagel exclaimed, "you have pledged yourself to fight. Your word and your honor are at stake. The fate of millions of men, the honor of the

---

* General Beck had sent Colonel Count Rudolf Marogna-Redwitz, a trusted member of the conspiracy, to Vienna to work with General von Knesebeck. The views of the Austrian anti-Nazis did not, however, agree with those of the Beck-Goerdeler group. The Austrian resistance was skeptical of certain military elements of the Beck-Goerdeler conspiracy and did not want Austria to remain within the Reich even with local autonomy. Ever since the Allied Moscow declaration of 1943, the Austrian resistance groups favored complete independence.

whole army, lie in your hands." For a moment Kluge did not answer, and then with an abrupt "No," he conducted Stülpnagel to his car. They did not shake hands as they finally parted.

Returning to the Hotel Raphael, Stülpnagel, before morning, was forced to release the imprisoned Nazis. Some of them had been locked in a room which had a radio, heard Hitler's broadcast to the German people, and thus learned of the plot's failure. Meanwhile, Kluge, who might still have saved the day in France, made a hasty declaration of faith in his Führer. "For us," he declared in an order of the day, "there will be no repetition of 1918, nor of the events in Italy." *

But these events in Paris were not yet known in Berlin. As night fell the plotters were still in control of the War Ministry. As a last desperate measure Gisevius suggested an attack on Goebbels' Propaganda office and the Gestapo headquarters in the Prinz Albrecht Strasse. Stauffenberg opposed such action. He was still confident the troops summoned to Berlin would arrive. At that moment the Berlin Commandant, Paul von Hase, had available thirty platoons composed of limited service men, used to guard buildings, offices and the Berlin Armory, and the Berlin Guard Battalion, a unit of the crack division *Gross Deutschland,* commanded by a Major Remer. Count von Helldorff had warned the con-

---

* Neither Stülpnagel nor Kluge had long to live. Ordered to Berlin, Stülpnagel realized the game was up. He drove to Verdun, the scene of Germany's great defeat in World War I. He stopped his car on the bank of the Meuse, got out, shot himself in the head and fell into the river, wounded but still alive. His chauffeur rescued him and took him to a hospital. There, blind and half dead, he was tortured and strangled to death. Kluge's eleventh-hour vacillation did not save him. He was too deeply implicated. This he realized when General Model, who had been appointed to succeed him, notified him of his dismissal in an abrupt telephone call, and told him to report to Hitler. After a futile attempt to surrender to General Patton's army somewhere in the Falaise Gap—whether before or after his dismissal I do not know—he boarded a plane at Paris, and on the flight to Metz took poison. Hitler ordered that the Field Marshal be buried without ceremony, and the few who knew the facts of his treason to the Führer were pledged to silence.

spirators against Remer, whom he knew to be an ardent Nazi, although not a party member. The conspirators had considered sending Remer on a military mission of some sort to Königsberg, where his family lived, on the day of the putsch. The idea was rejected because too many such "missions"—and quite a number had been arranged—would arouse suspicion. It was felt that Remer, a good soldier, would follow the orders of his superiors without question.

Remer was ordered to divide the Guard Battalion into thirty units, to occupy the Reich Chancellery, and to arrest a number of SS officers. He called his company commanders together and informed them of this order. He added that he doubted its authenticity and asked the lieutenants for their opinions. Among these lieutenants was one of the Nazi "guidance officers" (NSFO) that had been attached to each unit in the German army. Chosen from the ranks of fanatical party members, their function was to fan the flame of Nazism among the troops and to check on the commanders. This particular "guidance officer" had once been employed in the Propaganda Ministry and knew Goebbels. He offered to call Goebbels and inquire what was going on. Remer consented.

Goebbels already knew of what had happened and requested that Remer come to see him at once. Goebbels did not then know the origin or extent of the plot. Moreover, as a civilian he could not stop a regular army officer from executing a lawful order. Only Hitler himself could do that.

Goebbels received Remer coolly and informed him that he was obviously the victim of a "mystification" on the part of enemies of the state. He told Remer the Führer was very much alive and said he would prove it by calling Hitler on his direct wire. Remer would know his master's voice! Remer said later he was determined to arrest Goebbels if Hitler himself didn't speak on the phone. He wasn't thinking of politics or history but of inquiries and court-martials.

Hitler answered the telephone. He raged, ordered Remer to clean out the Replacement Army offices at once and gave the little major (who was afterwards promoted to major general) authority to "shoot as many people as he liked."

Remer was off at once. In his car he raced up and down the highways leading into Berlin ordering the approaching troops to halt. "Personal order of the Führer!" he yelled at the commanding officers, who were amazed to see a mere major rescinding orders issued by a general. There were arguments and disputes. The troops noticed something was wrong and became excited. There were shots. Some units continued to march, others halted at the city limits.

Meanwhile Goebbels urged the popular General Guderian, Inspector General of the Armored Divisions, to help stop all troop movements. Guderian had been informed of the conspiracy and had given his tacit approval. Goebbels' call convinced Guderian that the putsch, in which he knew many of his friends were involved, had failed. He might have helped save the day by directing the armored contingents against the SS. Instead he, too, raced about Berlin ordering approaching troops to turn back. On Fehrbelliner Platz he encountered the tank battalion of a Major Wolff about to bombard the SS headquarters. Guderian yelled: "Major, are you crazy? The Führer is still alive! Turn around and go home. You will only lose your head!" Major Wolff took his advice and ordered his battalion back to its quarters in Crampnitz. But the SS was faster. The party's elite troops arrived at Crampnitz ahead of the battalion, burned the barracks and killed the soldiers stationed there. The SS had fewer inhibitions than the army.

Count Helldorff, who apparently had heard from Goebbels, called the putsch headquarters about 7 o'clock and asked Gisevius to come and see him at once. As Gisevius left the War Ministry he met the first units of the Guard Regiment which had come, not to protect the conspirators, as Stauffenberg and Olbricht still believed, but to arrest them.

Colonel Jaeger, who had been assigned the job of arresting Goebbels, appeared at General von Hase's office on Unter den Linden at about the time Remer was talking to Goebbels and demanded troops to carry out his mission. Hase had none and had to ask Colonel Jaeger to wait.

Meanwhile, the news that Hitler was alive and would address the nation spread like wildfire throughout Berlin. At 8 o'clock the new Military District Commander, von Thüngen, began to crack under the strain and consulted with his subordinate, Hase, whether to go on with their part of the putsch. They decided to wait and see if Hitler would actually speak over the radio.

By 9 o'clock the Nazis had regained control of Berlin and General Reinicke, one of the most ruthless of the Nazi generals, under orders from Hitler and Keitel, had taken charge. He called up General von Hase and ordered all troops to be withdrawn or put under his command or he would assault the Bendlerstrasse. He did not realize how few forces the conspirators had there. Hase drove immediately to the Propaganda Ministry to find out what Remer was doing. Dr. Goebbels received him "cordially." He, Hase, could stay right there and await his arrest.

At 10 o'clock General Olbricht, still clutching at a hope he must have realized was receding forever, called his staff officers into his office and explained that since there were no soldiers he wanted *them* to guard the War Ministry building. No one was to leave or enter.

A Lieutenant Colonel Herder, who was not in on the conspiracy, spoke up and demanded:

"What in hell is going on anyway—who is guarding whom? What is this all about?"

Olbricht was forced to put his cards on the table. In an effort to gain the support of the staff of the Replacement

Army he made this impromptu speech: "Gentlemen, we have observed the situation at the front and at home with great misgivings for a long time. A great catastrophe is, without doubt, in the making. Measures had to be taken to prevent it. We are taking these measures now. I am asking you to assist me."

The officers left the room without committing themselves one way or the other.

A few minutes later shots were fired in the halls of the War Ministry. Beck, Olbricht, Haeften, Stauffenberg, Quirnheim and Lieutenant Klammroth were all in Hoeppner's office. Olbricht and Stauffenberg were busy on the telephone—Haeften went to see what was happening. The confusion was so great it was impossible to determine who was shooting and why. A group of officers with tommyguns and hand grenades forced their way into Hoeppner's office. A lieutenant colonel, Bodo von der Heyden, shouted:

"We are here to supply the front. This general order stops all supplies and replacements. Where is General Fromm?"

It was a mistake, perhaps equal to General Fellgiebel's failure to cut communications in East Prussia, that Fromm had not been shot by the conspirators. Von der Heyden, who demanded to see Fromm, was not shot either, but was politely told where the chief of the Replacement Army could be found. He departed and returned almost at once with his pistol drawn, accompanied by General Fromm and a group of officers who earlier had placed themselves at Beck's disposal. They had not been in the conspiracy, but had promised to support the putsch in the belief that Hitler was dead.

The conspirators had not only let Fromm live but, on his promise not to try to escape, had let him stay in his own apartment in the War Ministry. In some way he managed to contact some Nazi-dominated troops and ordered them to liberate him. No doubt he hoped he could exonerate himself in the eyes of his Führer if only he could execute the conspirators before they fell into party hands and implicated him. When Schlabrendorff saw him weeks later as a fellow prisoner of the Gestapo and obtained part of this story from him, he was still confident that his last-minute about-face would be rewarded by the Nazis and he would be spared. He was mistaken. He, too, was executed—but not before he had experienced the worst cruelties and indignities of which the system he helped to save was capable.

When Fromm entered Hoeppner's office he exclaimed: "Now I shall do to you exactly what you did to me this morning."

He asked the conspirators for their arms. Beck asked to keep his pistol, as he wished to use it on himself. Fromm consented, but asked Beck to act at once. According to Hoeppner's testimony, Beck started a sentence: "I recall the old times at this moment . . ." But Fromm interrupted and asked him to get on with the job. Beck said a few more words, then pointed the gun at himself and pulled the trigger. The bullet missed and hit the ceiling, wounding him only slightly. Fromm ordered his aides to Beck's assistance. "You better help the old man!"

Two officers rushed over to Beck, who had collapsed in his chair. While they took his weapon from him, Fromm addressed the others and said he would give them a few minutes to write farewell notes to their families. Hoeppner and Olbricht sat down to do so. Fromm left the room. The wounded Beck remained in his chair. In five minutes Fromm returned and urged Olbricht and Hoeppner to finish their letters in a hurry "so as not to make it too hard for the others." When they finished Fromm drew himself up and said: "In the name of the Führer, a summary court-martial, called by myself, has reached the following verdict: Colonel of the General Staff Merz von Quirnheim, General of the Infantry Olbricht, a man whose name I dare no longer utter

[Stauffenberg], and Lieutenant Werner von Haeften, are condemned to death."

He then ordered a lieutenant to take the condemned to the courtyard and execute them. The headlights of an armored car illuminated the scene. A detail from the *Gross Deutschland* Battalion fired the shots.

Of the conspirators who had been in Hoeppner's office that night only Beck and Hoeppner now remained. Fromm asked Hoeppner to follow him into another room where they could be alone. To Beck he said: "Now, how about it?" Beck asked for another pistol, which he was given. As Hoeppner left the room he heard the shot.

Fromm offered Hoeppner, "for friendship's sake," the privilege of suicide. But Hoeppner declined, saying, "I am not guilty in the same sense, and not a swine that I should have to judge myself." So, "as an old friend," Fromm had him taken to the army investigation prison. The Nazi People's Court, three weeks later, found Hoeppner guilty in the "same sense." I am sure that when he was tortured before he was hanged, Hoeppner regretted he had not availed himself of Fromm's offer.

The conspirators who had gathered in Stauffenberg's office were arrested between 10 and 11 o'clock. Yorck von Wartenburg, Fritz von der Schulenburg, Schwerin-Schwanenfeld, Stauffenberg's brother Berthold, Lieutenant Colonel Bernardis and Dr. Gerstenmaier were taken to the courtyard and were awaiting execution when the Gestapo arrived with orders that there were to be no more summary executions. Himmler wanted live prisoners from whom he could learn the names of other conspirators and all the details of their plot. The actual round-up of the conspirators Himmler entrusted to Scorzeny, the most ruthless of the SS hatchet men, and famous for his rescue of Mussolini.

The man hunt and terror began that night and by morning had spread over all Germany.

14. Conclusion

In March, 1945, shortly before the end of the war in Europe, as the German armies were retreating into the heart of Germany, Hitler ordered Albert Speer, the czar of the Nazi economy, to destroy Germany's railways and bridges, factories and public utilities, and to scorch the German earth. Speer recoiled before such an enormity and begged his Führer to consider what this would mean to future German generations. According to Speer's testimony at the Nürnberg trials, Hitler turned on him and said:

> If the war is to be lost, the nation perishes. This is inevitable. There is no necessity to consider what the people would require for even a primitive existence. On the contrary, it is wiser to destroy these things ourselves. For this nation has been proved the weaker, and the future belongs solely to the stronger Eastern nations. Besides, those who remain after the battle are the inferior ones. The good ones have fallen.

On one point Hitler was right, but not in the sense he intended it. The Gestapo terror, particularly the terror following July 20, had taken a heavy toll of the Germans needed in the work of regeneration. In this way Hitler did indeed work for the fulfillment of his prophecy that the nation was to perish. If he could not lead, he tried to see to it that Germany should have no leadership.

When, after the end of the war, I began to assemble the data about the German underground which I had been collecting since 1943, I had only a limited objective in mind —to tell the story of a group of men and women within Germany who had had the courage to conspire against Hitler, and how they did so. But as the work progressed it became evident that the history of this conspiracy illuminates one of the fundamental issues of our generation.

It reveals how the various strata of German society reacted when a dictator set out to destroy democracy. In Germany, at least, there were no defenses in depth against totalitarian attack. When the line was broken at a vital point, the battle was lost. It should make all of us consider how adequate our own institutions are for democracy's preservation and how far its survival must depend upon the devotion to these institutions of men and women ready and willing to act *in time* to defend them.

The anatomy of dictatorship is laid bare in the German documents now available to us, especially in the voluminous record of the Nürnberg trial. Here we have an unprecedented opportunity to study the totalitarian technique and to learn lessons for our own defense. Even this brief study of the German underground gives some clues.

The fatal weakness of the political system of the Weimar Republic lay in the ease with which absolute power could be taken from the people and entrusted to one man. When constitutional safeguards are so frail that a single thrust can overcome them, the people may be deprived even of the opportunity to make an effective fight to preserve democracy. Yet today in many European countries there are bitter struggles over inserting in the new constitutions the checks and balances that delimit political power. These checks and balances may at times seem frustrating, and appear to make democracy less efficient than dictatorship. But they are really beyond price.

The truth of this is proven by the German story. Under Hitler political parties melted away. Organized labor, at first seduced by demagogic promises, was later strong-armed into submission. The intellectuals and business and professional men retired in dismay and fear into their work. The army came to heel. The churches remained, but in the political sphere were ineffective. And the sum total was disaster for Germany, leaving a problem in political and economic reconstruction to test man's skill and ingenuity.

Seventy million Germans lie between Russia and what we call the Western World. If these Germans become the tool of either East or West against the other, there is no basis for peace in Europe or the world. If they remain an idle and recalcitrant element there can be no lasting economic recovery in Europe.

Since the days of Bismarck the Germans have too often been a wayward and dangerous element, with victory more arrogant and with defeat subtly dangerous. And now total collapse followed by military occupation and the narrowing of the German *Lebensraum* have accentuated the German problem. We, the victors, have crowded the Germans together in an area which does not today, and will not in the immediate future, have the resources to keep them fed or usefully employed. Despair, hunger and idleness threaten to breed new and dangerous doctrines, and military impotence alone will not prevent this situation from becoming an actual threat to the peace. Bitterness and resentment, bred of defeat and intolerable living conditions which should have turned the people's hatred against Hitler and the Nazis who caused it all, are likely to be visited upon the powers in occupation. People everywhere, particularly the young, blame their miseries upon the men they see in control, not upon their predecessors, even though the latter are the true culprits.

Those who expect the great majority of the German people to accept defeat, admit their collective guilt and rise up tomorrow as trusted members of a democratic and peaceful European society, are deluding themselves—they are deluding themselves both as regards the national characteristics of the Germans and as regards the manner in which human beings, German or non-German, react to conditions such as those in Germany. It is equally naïve to expect much from programs of re-education imposed by a military occupation.

The Germans, themselves, will have to take the vital decision to break with the past—the past of Bismarck and of the Kaiser and that far more sordid past of the Hitler regime. But in trying to break with all that is warped in this past, the Germans will naturally hope to find somewhere in their own history those better traditions which can serve as a guide in the work of regeneration. Here may lie the value of the evidence that even in the blackest Hitler days there was a better strain which, though submerged and often relatively powerless, was not entirely crushed. This strain, based largely on the Christian impulse, is represented by those German men and women who took part in the struggle against the Nazis for the sake of principle.

It is easy to criticize the German underground for its delays, disunities, vacillations, and ultimate failure. But in a police state such as Hitler and Himmler organized it is not likely that men will do much better than a Beck, a Goerdeler, a Moltke, a Leuschner or a Stauffenberg.

For the future of Germany there is some hope because Germans from within the Reich made the attempt to rid the world of Hitler. Upon their example and their ideas the Germans can build, if they choose the road to democracy.

END

INDEX

Index

Gruhn, Erna, 40
Guderian, Colonel General Heinz, 53, 63, 190
Gürtner, Franz, 112
Guttenberg, Baron Karl Ludwig von, 34

Habermann, Max, 34
Haeften, Hans Bernd von, 170
Haeften, Lieutenant Werner von, 7, 170, 182, 185, 192, 194
Hague Convention, 87
Halder, General Franz, 38, 41, 42, 43, 45, 48, 49, 50, 52, 54, 57, 59, 62, 75, 98, 133, 134, 149
Halifax, Viscount, 86
Hammerstein-Equord, Colonel General Kurt von, 15, 24, 25, 26, 53, 106, 107, 109
Hammerstein - Equord, Lieutenant Ludwig von, 185
Hansen, Colonel Georg, 80
Harnack, Otto, 101
Hase, Lieutenant General Paul von, 178, 185, 188, 191
Hassell, Ulrich von, 24, 27, 28, 34, 49, 51, 54, 57, 62, 63, 64, 153, 156, 181
Haubach, Theodor, 103, 104, 105, 108, 118, 167, 181
Haushofer, Albrecht, 34, 122, 123, 124
Helldorff, Count Wolf Heinrich von, 140, 154, 160, 179, 185, 188, 190
Henderson, Sir Nevile, 16, 21, 27, 51
Henk, Emil, 167
Herder, Colonel, 191
Hermes, Andreas, 34
Hess, Rudolf, 19, 122, 123, 127
Heusinger, Lieutenant General Adolf, 6
Heyden, Lieutenant Colonel Bodo von der, 192
Heydrich, Reinhard, 73, 74, 75
Hilferding, Rudolf, 102
Hilfrich, Bishop, 118
Himmler, Heinrich, 3, 6, 9, 11, 15, 20, 40, 47, 55, 70, 71, 72, 75, 76, 78, 79, 80, 91, 123, 127, 133, 135, 141, 142, 145, 147 ff, 194, 198
Hindenburg, Oskar von, 13

Hindenburg, Paul von, 13, 26, 31, 111; will of, 37
Hitler, Adolf, injuries suffered July 20, 8; oath to, 37; order to attack Poland, 51; radio address, July 20, 1944, 1, 2; speech of, September 26, 1938, 45; speech to generals, August 1939, 50; speech to generals, November 23, 1939, 56; takes command of Russian front, 63
Hoare, Sir Samuel (Viscount Templewood), 146
Hoegner, Wilhelm, 102
Hoeppner, Colonel General Erich, 45, 53, 83, 178, 182, 184, 185, 186, 187, 192, 193, 194
Hoernle, Erwin, 99
Hofacker, Lieutenant Colonel Caesar von, 176, 187
Holland. See Netherlands
Huber, Karl, 121, 122
Hugenberg, Alfred, 14, 31, 35, 112

Institute for Pacific Relations, 89
International Labor Office, 106
International Military Tribunals. See Nürnberg Trials
International Transport Workers Union, 97, 103

Jackson, Justice Robert H., 25, 127
Jacob, Franz, 173, 174
Jaeger, Colonel, 191
Jay, John, 88
Jessen, Jens Peter, 27, 28, 29, 33, 149, 153, 156, 157, 161, 162
Jodl, General Alfred, 6, 59

Kaiser, Jakob, 107, 181
Kaltenbrunner, Ernst, 73, 80, 163
Keitel, Field Marshal Wilhelm, 6, 7, 10, 15, 47, 50, 51, 53, 59, 65, 74, 75, 79, 177, 183, 187, 191
Kerrl, Hanns, 110
Kessel, Albrecht von, 54, 75, 132
Kesselring, Field Marshal Albert, 39
Kiep, Otto C., 87, 88, 135
Klammroth, Lieutenant Colonel Bernard, 192
Kleist, Ewald von, 69, 185

Obersalzberg, 139
OKW (*Oberkommando der Wehrmacht*, Supreme Command of the Armed Forces), 15, 64, 70
Olbricht, General Friedrich, 25, 33, 64, 67, 115, 140, 154, 160, 162, 178, 181, 182, 183, 184, 185, 191, 192, 193
Oppen, Georg von, 185
OSS (Office of Strategic Services), 127
Oster, Major General Hans, 25, 42, 44, 45, 46, 47, 50, 54, 58, 59, 60, 61, 62, 64, 71, 76, 78, 80, 127, 129, 134, 135, 175, 181

Papen, Franz von, 13, 14, 30, 31, 35, 37, 98, 105, 111, 122
Patton, General George S., Jr., 188
Paulus, Field Marshal Friedrich von, 62, 65, 66, 172
People's Court (*Volksgerichtshof*), 68, 82, 83, 162, 194
Perth, Lord, 46
Phillips, William, 27
Pieck, Wilhelm, 99
Pieckenbrock, Colonel, 74
Planck, Erwin, 146, 156, 157, 162
Poland, invasion of, 50, 52, 76, 78
Pölchau, Harald, 118
Polish Corridor, 19
Popitz, Johannes, 24, 27, 28, 29, 33, 34, 62, 123, 147, 149, 150, 162; indictment of, 151 ff.
Preysing, Cardinal von, 117, 119
Pringsheim, Fritz, 148

Quirnheim, Colonel Merz von, 182, 183, 192, 193

Rastenburg, 3, 9
Reckzeh, Dr., 88
Reichenau, General Walter von, 35, 37, 53
Reichsbanner, 104
Reichsführer-SS. *See* Himmler
Reichsrat, 95
Reichsschrifttumskammer (Nazi Writers Association), 20
Reichssicherheitshauptamt. See Central Security Office

Reichstag, 95, 99, 107, 182; burning of, 20, 55, 98, 148; elections, November 1932, 12; elections, March 5, 1933, 14; exclusion of Communists from, 14
Reichwein, Adolf, 105, 173, 174
Reinicke, General, 191
Remer, Major, 188, 189, 191
Remmele, Ernst, 99
Replacement Army (*Ersatzheer*), 2, 4, 5, 25, 33, 64, 69, 140, 177, 178, 179, 183, 184, 190, 192
Rhineland, occupation of, 36, 39
Rhodes Foundation, 89
Rhodes scholarships, 87, 88
Ribbentrop, Joachim von, 9, 10, 27, 28, 40, 46, 48, 50, 51, 75, 122, 153, 154, 156, 159
Ritter, Gerhard, 122
Roeder, 79
Roesch, Fr., S.J., 118
Röhm, Ernst, 10, 37, 150; purge, 15, 36, 37
Rommel, Field Marshal Erwin, 3, 139, 176, 177, 180
Rose-Innes, Dorothy, 85
Rosenberg, Alfred, 110
Rote Kapelle, 79, 100, 101
Ruhr industrialists, 14
Rundstedt, Field Marshal Karl Rudolf Gert von, 35, 60, 136, 176
Russia. *See* U.S.S.R.

S.A. (*Sturmabteilung*, Storm Troopers), 18, 31, 37, 104
Sack, Dr. Carl, 79
Saefkow, Anton, 173, 174
Sarre, Marie-Louise, 148, 162, 163, 164
Sas, Colonel G. J., 58, 59, 60, 61
Schacht, Dr. Hjalmar, 13, 14, 31, 40, 44, 45, 49, 77, 78, 112, 127, 145
Scheliha, Dolf von, 101
Schieffelin, William J., 89
Schlabrendorff, Fabian von, 25, 51, 53, 57, 62, 63, 64, 66, 67, 68, 71, 78, 144, 145, 193
Schleicher, General Kurt von, 15, 30, 35, 37
Schleicher, Rüdiger, 76